Children as trophies?

Examining the evidence on same-sex parenting

Patricia Morgan

CHRISTIAN INFLUENCE IN A SECULAR WORLD

The Christian Institute

D0412748

"I'm not in favour of gay couples seeking to adopt children because I question whether that is the right start in life. We should not see children as trophies.

Children, in my judgement, and I think it's the judgement of almost everyone including single parents, are best brought up where you have two natural parents in a stable relationship. There's no question about that. What we know from the evidence is that, generally speaking, that stability is more likely to occur where the parents are married than where they are not."

The Rt Hon Jack Straw MP on the *Today* programme, 4 November 1998

First printed in 2002

ISBN 1 901086 18 6

Published by The Christian Institute
26 Jesmond Road, Newcastle upon Tyne, NE2 4PQ

Cover Image of girl:
Digital Imagery© copyright 2001 PhotoDisc, Inc.
Image posed by model and is used for illustrative purposes only

Designed by Mike Judge, The Christian Institute.
Printed by Creative Print and Design Group, Saxon Way, Harmondsworth, Middlesex, UB7 0LW

Contents

About the author

Acknowledgement

Foreword by Colin Hart

About the author

Patricia Morgan, Senior Research Fellow at the Institute for the Study of Civil Society, is a sociologist specialising in family policy and criminology. Her books include *Delinquent Fantasies*, 1978; *Facing up to family income*, 1989; *Families in Dreamland*, 1992; *Farewell to the Family?*, 1995; *Are Families Affordable?*, 1996; *Who needs parents?*, 1996; *Adoption and the Care of Children*, 1998; *Adoption: The Continuing Debate*, 1999; and *Marriage-Lite*, 2000. She has contributed chapters to many other books, as well as articles for periodicals and national newspapers.

Acknowledgement

The author wishes to thank Humphrey Dobson, Dr Oluseyi Hotonu and Rachel Woodward for their assistance in preparing the text for publication.

Foreword

"I'm not in favour of gay couples seeking to adopt children because I question whether that is the right start in life. We should not see children as trophies.

Children in my judgement, and I think it's the judgement of almost everyone including single parents, are best brought up where you have two natural parents in a stable relationship. There's no question about that. What we know from the evidence is that, generally speaking, that stability is more likely to occur where the parents are married than where they are not."[1]

The Rt Hon Jack Straw MP, on the *Today* programme, 4 November 1998

In 1995 Essex Social Services rejected a request to adopt a child from millionaire homosexual businessmen Barrie Drewitt and Tony Barlow.[2]

Four years later in December 1999 a surrogate mother bore twins for the same two men who had paid £200,000 to a Los Angeles gay surrogate agency. Both men had provided sperm used to fertilise donor eggs in a laboratory. The embryos were then implanted in the surrogate mother's womb. It is a biological fact that a child can only have one father, but a US court decided that the twins each had two fathers. This was despite the fact that DNA testing had revealed which was the true father of each twin. The birth certificates were amended accordingly.

The Bishop of Southwark responded by saying:

> "It's adults designing children for the benefit of adults. We are producing a generation of children mixed up and insecure, not because they are wanting for nothing in a material sense, but because they are totally confused about their identity, because family life is in turmoil."[3]

According to press reports, the millionaire gay couple now plan to have yet another child.[4]

When Jack Straw, the then Home Secretary, was asked on the *Today* programme whether he was in favour of gay adoption, he said he was not because "we should not see children as trophies". He argued that children are not trophies. They are not to be 'awarded' to homosexual couples merely to enhance the status of homosexuality.

Some homosexuals – male and female – may genuinely want children. But this desire, however strongly felt, does not constitute a right to have children. The desires of adults must not determine the decisions made about placing children for adoption.

More positively, Jack Straw argued that the best interests of children demand a mother and a father in a stable relationship. This is most likely to occur in marriage.

The best interests of children

Until very recently the general assumption has been that marriage is the ideal environment for raising children. So children awaiting placement for adoption, just as much as other children, deserve the best, the ideal: to be brought up by a married couple.

Under UK law only married couples or single people can adopt children. Whilst adoption by single people is not the norm, it can have a place particularly when a child has been abused or suffered disruption from multiple foster placements.

Adoption by homosexual couples remains illegal. But social services and the courts are using the vehicle of single person adoption to get round the law. Children have been placed for adoption with a single person, in the full knowledge that that person is cohabiting with someone of the same sex.

Gay rights groups and sympathetic researchers claim that the best interests of the child may mean placing the child with homosexuals. For example: "[T]he evidence to date suggests that home environments provided by gay and lesbian parents are as likely as those provided by heterosexual parents to support and to enable children's psychosocial growth."[5]

In 1999 this view found support from Dame Butler-Sloss, President of the Family Division of the High Court.[6] But as long ago as 1991, British Agencies for Adoption and Fostering (BAAF) made clear their support for adoption by homosexuals.[7]

Today several social services departments in England are actively recruiting homosexuals to adopt and foster children.[8] Indeed, support for homosexual adoption is now unquestioned in social work orthodoxy.

A radical change from current practice

Support for homosexual adoption may be unquestioned within social work, but such placements seem to be rare in practice.

Every year around 4,000 children are adopted. Most of these are adoptions of children who are looked after by a local authority. In 2000/2001 there were 3,100 adoptions of children from care.[9]

The evidence is that the overwhelming majority of adoption placements from care are still with married couples. In a recent study published by BAAF using 1998/99 data from 80 per cent of local authorities it was found that 95 per cent of children were placed with married parents, with five per cent placed with single parents.[10]

When the Government announced its plans to review the adoption law, official sources downplayed claims that the new Adoption Bill would make it easier for homosexuals to adopt. Subsequent newspaper reports on the announcement quoted a 1998 study which found that only three adoptions in that year were by homosexuals.[11]

Although adoption by homosexual couples may be rare, fostering by homosexuals is more common.

Official statistics show that for all the high public profile surrounding gay rights, there are remarkably few homosexual couples. The Labour Force Survey of autumn 1999 reported that 0.2 per cent of households in Great Britain are composed of people who consider themselves to be a 'same-sex couple'.[12]

Moreover though homosexual adoption is not particularly questioned within social work, it certainly is outside. Even those who are liberal on gay rights balk at the prospect of adoption by homosexuals. There is a deep unease amongst the public.

British Social Attitudes last asked the public their views on homosexual adoption in 1993. They found that 74 per cent of the public oppose adoption by lesbians and 84 per cent oppose adoption by male homosexuals.[13]

Whatever the level of public disapproval or the actual number of homosexual adoptions which take place every year, one thing is clear: Homosexual adoption and fostering represents a massive change in public policy.

Homosexual adoption profoundly challenges the globally held assumption that children need a mother *and* a father. As Patricia Morgan points out: "If the development of children born into lesbian mother homes is demonstrably normal, then this challenges the need for fathers, and questions whether a male and female parent are at all necessary or desirable for children's development." In the same way adoption by male homosexuals challenges the need for mothers.

The Judaeo-Christian ethic

Homosexual adoption is radically opposed to the Judaeo-Christian family ethic which views marriage as the only right context for sexual relations and the procreation of children.[14]

The Genesis account states "For this reason a man shall leave his father and mother and be united to his wife, and they will become one flesh."[15] Parenthood is male and female. Children need male and female role models. The fifth of the Ten Commandments enshrines this.[16]

In Christian understanding, children are not possessions but a gift from God. There is no 'right' to have children. To "Be fruitful and multiply"[17] is the normal expectation of marriage, though it is recognised that not all married couples can have children.

Having children is one of the three purposes of marriage universally recognised by all Christian Churches.[18]

Procreation is tied to marriage. Children are not to be spawned in random relations, but begotten in arrangements in which their parents are bound to their offspring by the ties of law as well as nature.[19] The intention is for parents to be as committed to the nurture of their children as they are committed to each other as husband and wife.

The Western legal tradition

Adoption is not a modern idea. Historically where adoption has been codified in law it has usually been for the purposes of the adopter, not the adoptee. No doubt in practice many less formal arrangements were made. In Graeco-Roman times adoption law was related to the need for a male heir. Adoption also occurred in Babylonian, Hindu, Egyptian and Chinese cultures. Elizabeth Cole and Kathryn Donley conclude that in early history:

> "...the primary purpose of adoption was to serve adult interests rather than child interests. If a child benefited it was a secondary gain. Certainly the concept of the 'best interests of the child' was not paramount, if indeed it

was given any weight at all. Most European countries, with the exception of England, built their law upon the Roman and later Napoleonic codes." [20]

The issue of inheritance still dominated in the Napoleonic law which included the requirement that the adopter be aged over 50 and be sterile.

In England inheritance was a secondary consideration. The issue of inheritance was addressed in the 1926 Adoption of Children Act and subsequently in the 1969 Act.[21] It was only addressed because it was for the benefit of the adoptee, not because of the issue of continuing the family line. In the USA the legal tradition followed the practice in England[22] which was not based on the formal Graeco-Roman model of adoption.

Prior to the 1926 Act adoptions were informally carried out between families. As Brenda Hoggett (now Lady Justice Hale) states :

"There was no regulation of adoption placement and the adoption order did little more than give legal sanction to the de facto transfer which had already been agreed. The court's role was limited to checking that the birth parents had indeed agreed and that the child's welfare did not suffer."[23]

In the debates leading up to the 1926 Act many of the Christian voluntary agencies were cautious about more state involvement in adoption. The adoption of babies dominated adoption until the 1970s.

The role of Christian agencies in adoption and fostering remained strong until local authorities were *required,* rather than just permitted, to establish adoption services in 1975.[24] In tandem with this fewer babies were given up for adoption as single parenthood become more socially acceptable and abortion more widely available.

As Stephen Cretney points out

"Traditionally adoption services were provided by voluntary agencies – often with a religious inspiration – but the Children Act 1975 imposed on every local authority a duty to establish and maintain a comprehensive adoption service…"[25]

"Until 1982 there was nothing to stop private individuals (such as doctors or the matrons of maternity homes) from arranging adoption placements; but it is now a criminal offence for anyone other than an adoption agency to make arrangements for the adoption of a child or to place a child for adoption."[26]

Today adoption agencies are deemed in the legislation to be either a local authority or a Government approved adoption society. All adoptions except those by relatives must go through an adoption agency.

The Christian stake in adoption and fostering

Christian involvement in adoption and fostering is rooted in some central Christian beliefs. Adoption is a theological concept central to the Bible.[27] The Apostle Paul would have been well aware of Roman Adoption Law with its primary function to guard the line of inheritance. In deliberate contrast to this Paul argues that all Christian believers, male *and female*, are adopted as sons into God's family.[28] Believers so adopted have the full rights as sons.[29] Paul taught that this adoption is made possible only by Christ's sacrifice of himself on the cross in our place, as the substitute for our sins. As Christ said: "Greater love hath no man than this, that a man lay down his life for his friends".[30]

Christians are to show this same love towards their neighbours because they themselves are beneficiaries of God's love in being adopted as sons. This is a very strong motivation to care for children in need, particularly for those who have no parents.

The New Testament commends caring for orphans and widows as "pure and faultless" religion.[31] In the 18th and 19th centuries Christians set up many orphanages. The diaries of the itinerant evangelists John Wesley and George Whitefield are peppered with references to the setting up and maintenance of orphanages.

Commenting on efforts in the nineteenth century to help the destitute, John Stroud made the following observation:

"Today, we are so used to calling upon the government to deal with this or that problem that it is surprising to realise that for a large part of Victoria's reign, nearly half of it, there was strong opposition to Government 'interference' with any part of social life. Nor did action come from the churches, as organised bodies. Action came first from individuals, usually members of the churches, usually members of the evangelical wings "[32]

The most prominent such individual was Dr. Barnardo. Although he is best known for his children's homes, it is less well known that he enthusiastically set up what were known as 'boarding-out' schemes. These pioneered the shift away from residential child care. The 'boarded-out' children were placed with carefully chosen foster parents and they stayed with that family until leaving home for work or to get married, just as the natural children of the family.[33] As Dr. Barnardo said in 1904:

"Still, although our families [children's homes] are so good…there is something better – boarding-out, because it gives them the natural instead of the artificial, and then it gives the family instead of the institution. 'He setteth the solitary in families,' [Psalm 68:6] and we cannot do better than imitate the Divine order and let every child who can be brought up in a family be so brought up, and give it family life, and family love…"[34]

Christian agencies back homosexual adoption

Even today most of the large charities involved with adoption and fostering have Christian roots. This is the case with Barnardo's, the Children's Society and NCH Action for Children whose respective theological roots are evangelical, Church of England and Methodist.

Despite this all of these Christian charities now embrace homosexual adoption.

In 1994 Barnardo's changed their trust deed so that the requirement for children to be brought up only in the Protestant faith in accordance with the Bible was replaced by a weaker wording.[35]

NCH Action for Children was founded in 1869 by a Methodist Minister. The organisation now states "Both our Methodist roots and over 130 years of work inform our values as a charity. We are committed to equality and diversity, to social justice and to helping every child and young person to reach their unique potential".[36]

In 1993 the Methodist Conference passed contradictory motions affirming Church teaching that sex was only for marriage, but also affirming the ministry of lesbians and gay men within the Church.[37]

Barnardo's and NCH had both accepted homosexual adoption by 1990.[38] At that time the Children's Society maintained that homosexual adoption was inconsistent with its Christian trust deed.

The policy changed in 1999 without the agreement of the Charity's Patrons, the Archbishops of Canterbury and York, and despite the fact that the society only placed 16 children a year for adoption or fostering. The Society even cited the 1998 Lambeth Conference resolution in support of their action. But whilst it is true that the resolution affirms that all are "loved by God" whatever their sexuality, the resolution also affirms that:

- Homosexual practice is incompatible with the Bible;
- Christians can experience same-sex attraction and that the Church should seek sensitively to minister to such people;
- For those not called to marriage sexual abstinence is the right course; and that same-sex unions are to be rejected.

Only the evangelical and the large Roman Catholic agencies now resist homosexual fostering and adoption.

Secular values and social work

If the Christian adoption agencies have been pushed into political correctness, even more so have social work departments. Adoption itself has been stigmatised.

It is now widely accepted that over "the past 20 years or so, there has been a negative culture in social work in relation to adoption...".[39] The Prime Minister himself has argued that "too often in the past adoption has been seen as a last resort".[40]

It is a hopeful sign that the Government acknowledges that the care system has not been a good parent to the children for whom it has been providing substitute care.[41] Under six per cent of looked after children were adopted in 2000/2001.[42] This figure is lamentably low.

It is ironic that though social workers may strongly disagree about the value of adoption, they are completely united on the 'right' of homosexual couples to be able to adopt children. Fortunately such secular political correctness has not as yet been fully put into practice. When it comes to adoption the overwhelming majority of placements are with married couples.

Things may not stay this way if influential people within adoption and fostering achieve their goal of giving unmarried couples the right to adopt. In BAAF's own study of adoption placements 95 per cent of the children were placed with married couples. Despite this BAAF argue that "in the light of the major alteration in patterns of family life in the UK since the 1960s" it is time to reconsider the legal ban on unmarried couples jointly adopting.[43]

In the present *Adoption and Children Bill* BAAF are lobbying for homosexual couples "in a stable union" to be able to adopt.[44] They argue that assessment for adoption placements must focus on the "strength and stability of the relationship between the two adults as a critical factor..."[45]

Susanna Cheal, Chief Executive of the charity *Who Cares? Trust*, puts it another way: "It does not really matter what the configuration of people is. It is the quality of the relationship with the prospective parents that matters."[46] To assert that "It does not really matter what the configuration of people is" is a claim of colossal proportions.

As Patricia Morgan points out

"This amounts to more than a matter of simple tolerating 'diversity', since human history, anthropology and, above all, biology, provide us with no precedents for a 'family' with two men or two women at its nucleus. To avoid discrimination, the law must now undo handicaps present in nature…"

The 'pick and mix family' where any configuration of adults will do is also a flagrant rejection of the very Judaeo-Christian beliefs which pioneered adoption and fostering in the UK.

Children as trophies?

Social work's stated concern is to act in the best interests of the child. Most concerned with adoption placements would admit that ultimately that question should be decided by the evidence.

To go against the evidence would be to make children the subject of their adopter's interests and not their own. They could indeed become 'trophies'.

Patricia Morgan has looked at the evidence in meticulous detail. She has produced what is the most comprehensive review of research on same-sex parenting ever published in Europe.

The evidence is very clear for any who wish to consider it.

Colin Hart
Director, The Christian Institute
December 2001

Endnotes:

1   *The Independent*, 5 November 1998; *The Herald*, 5 November 1998
2   *The Daily Telegraph*, 28 October 1999
3   *Reuters News Service*, 28 October 1999
4   E.g.: *Daily Telegraph*, 1 June 2000
5   Patterson, C J and Redding, R E, 'Lesbian and Gay Families with Children: Implications of Social Science Research for Policy', *Journal of Social Issues*, 52(3), 1996, page 43
6   *The Independent*, 16 October 1999
7   See *BAAF Adoption and Fostering News*, January/February 1991
8   Newham Social Services advertised for fosterers in *The Pink Paper* 5 October 2001. In April 2000 Newcastle Social Services placed an advertisement for potential gay adopters in the gay section of a regional magazine; Rotherham Social Services advertised for potential homosexual foster parents: see *The Daily Telegraph* 21 September 1996
9   House of Commons, Hansard, 6 November 2001, col. 230 wa
10 Surveying Adoption : A comprehensive analysis of local authority adoptions 1998/1999, BAAF, 2000
11 *The Sunday Times*, 23 April 2000; *The Express*, 24 April 2000; *The Mirror*, 24 April 2000
12 House of Commons, Hansard, 11 May 2000, col. 471 wa
    (Cohabiting with same-sex refers to same sex couples and not siblings or platonic friends)
13 Jowell, R et al, *British Social Attitudes (The 11th Report)*, Dartmouth Publishing, 1994, page 196
14 See Leviticus 18:22; Romans 1:26-27; Matthew 5:27-28; 1 Corinthians 6:9
15 Genesis 2:24 (NIV)
16 Exodus 20:12
17 Genesis 1:28 (AV)
18 The others being the mutual society, help and comfort of man and wife and as a remedy against sin.
19 Arkes, H, 'Homosexuality and the Law' in Wolfe, C (Ed.) *Homosexuality and American Public Life*, Spence, 1999, page 177
20 Cole, E and Donley, K S, 'History, Values and Placement Policy Issues in Adoption' in Brodzinsky, D M and Schechter, M D (Eds.) *The Psychology of Adoption*, Oxford University Press, 1990, page 274
21 *Ibid*, pages 274-275

22 *Ibid*, page 274

23 Hoggett, B, 'Adoption Law: an Overview' in Bean, P (Ed.) *Adoption- Essays in Social Policy, Law and Sociology*, Tavistock Publications, 1984, page 132

24 Holman B, *The Corporate Parent- Manchester Children's Department 1948-1971*, National Institute for Social Work, 1996, pages 11, 12, 96. The 1948 Children Act established children's departments in every local authority. Their essential role was not as a provider of adoption services, but to monitor the child's welfare between being placed initially with his prospective adoptive parents and an adoption order being made by the court. The departments performed this role with a fairly light touch. In addition, the courts often appointed the Children's Officer as the guardian ad litem (independent supervisor) who would assess the suitability of the adoption and provide a court report before the adoption order was made.

25 Cretney, S, *Elements of Family Law*, Sweet & Maxwell, 1992, page 230

26 *Ibid*, page 233

27 In the Old Testament there was no provision for adoption to continue the family line. Other means were provided, including the duty on a man to take his brother's widow as his own wife where his brother had died childless. See Deuteronomy 25 and Lyall, F, 'Roman Law in the Writings of Paul – Adoption', *Journal of Biblical Literature*, 88, 1969, page 459

The concept of adoption is present in the Old Testament in two ways. First Israel is adopted as God's first born. (Isaiah 1:2, Jeremiah 3·19, Hosea 11:1). The prophets later made clear that Israel was God's first born. Second, the Jewish people understood that God adopted King David's line as anointed Royal sons and heirs. So strong is this adoption that Psalm 2 speaks of David being "begotten".

28 All believers – male and female – are sons of God. There is neither Jew nor Greek, slave nor free, male nor female. All are heirs according to promise. See Galatians 3:26-29

29 The crucial distinction between Roman law and the Judeo-Christian tradition is central to the Apostle Paul's theological arguments. In the Jewish custom adoption meant conferring the benefits of the family on the adoptee. The enjoyment of the rights began immediately. The adoptee was treated as a son, not a slave. In the same way Christian believers are adopted by God with the "full rights as sons". In the Passover the first born son of every Egyptian family died, but the households of the Israelites were spared from

death by the blood of the lamb. The whole of Israel was God's first born son (Exodus 4:22). The New Testament makes clear that Christ was the lamb of God (John 1:36, 1 Corinthians 5:7, Revelation chapters 14-21). Christ's sacrifice of himself on the cross is compared by Paul to be like redeeming someone from slavery to sonship. See Galatians 4:5. The same word for adoption – *huiothesia* – is also used in Ephesians 1:5 and Romans 8:23. So strong is this adopted bond that Galatians 4:6 teaches that Christian believers cry out in their hearts "Abba", the Aramaic word for "Daddy".

[30]   John 15:13 (AV)

[31]   James 1:27 (NIV)

[32]   Stroud, J, *Thirteen Penny Stamps, The Story of the Church of England Children's Society (Waifs and Strays) from 1881 to the 1970s*, Hodder and Stoughton, 1971, page 8

[33]   Mrs. Barnardo and Marchant, J, *The Memoirs of the late Dr. Barnardo*, Hodder and Stoughton, 1907, page 185-203

[34]   *Ibid*, page 196

[35]   Oakes, G, *Christianity and Barnardos, Memorandum & Articles of Association* (private paper). The original requirement that children "be brought up…only in the Protestant faith according to the text and doctrine of the Holy Scriptures…" by 1994 had become "[the] promotion among children and young people of the knowledge of the Christian faith or the faith in which they were brought up…having regard to (the Association's) Protestant history and its Christian inspiration…"

[36]   See http://www.nch.org.uk/aboutnch/index.asp?filename=\flatfiles\aboutnch/methodist.html as at 25 November 2001

[37]   See *The Guardian*, 30 June 1993

[38]   Letter from the Director of operations of the NCH to The Christian Institute, 5 November 1990; Letter from the Director of Child Care of Barnardo's to The Christian Institute, 30 October 1990

[39]   House of Commons, Hansard, Adoption and Children Bill Special Standing Committee, Third Sitting, 21 November 2001 (morning), col. 133

[40]   *The Guardian*, 8 July 2000

[41]   House of Commons, Hansard, Adoption and Children Bill Special Standing Committee, Third Sitting, 21 November 2001 (morning), col. 130

[42]   House of Commons, Hansard, 6 November 2001, col. 230 wa

[43]   BAAF *Memorandum of Evidence to the House of Commons Select Committee on the Adoption and Children Bill*, BAAF, 27 April 2001

44 House of Commons, Hansard, Adoption and Children Bill Special Standing Committee, Second Sitting, 20 November 2001, col. 40
45 *Loc cit*
46 House of Commons, Hansard, Adoption and Children Bill Special Standing Committee, Third Sitting, 21 November 2001 (morning), col. 160

Chapter 1
Homosexuals and parenthood

Gay activists are demanding the complete equalisation of all 'family forms'. This demand is being made at a time of considerable family change. Behind it lies more than many realise: full equivalent rights for same-sex couples, homosexual adoptive parents, and homosexual individuals seeking to adopt children or become parents by means of assisted reproduction, along with full access to surrogacy and donor insemination.

For obvious reasons, adoption and surrogacy are going to rank higher on the agenda of prospective homosexual parents, than they would for heterosexuals, who are not limited to these means for acquiring children.[1] However, questions of marriage for gays and lesbians, or rights to adoption for same-sex couples, arise not just because gays and lesbians are anxious to marry and parent. They have an importance strategically, in that they involve the law in underwriting and elevating same-sex relationships as completely 'normal', or equally legitimate and acceptable in every sense to male and female relationships.

UK law – as it is and might be

At present, same-sex couples cannot jointly adopt children as married, heterosexual couples can. An unmarried couple, whether they are heterosexual or homosexual, cannot adopt jointly as a couple so the application has to be made on a single basis by only one of the partners. The rationale behind this policy is that two people should make a commitment to each other before making the commitment to the child. The formal relationship between the parties cannot exist through the child alone. The higher courts in England and Wales, and Scotland, have decided that sexual orientation does not in itself make an applicant unsuitable for single person adoption. There are a very small number of cases where the courts have allowed single person adoption to take place in the full knowledge that the adopter was cohabiting with someone of the same sex. The fostering guidelines to the Children Act 1989, imply that lesbians and male homosexuals can apply to be foster parents using the same criteria as anybody else.

Only a biological mother and father have any legal status in relation to a child. A 'partner' who is not biologically related to the child does not. However an unmarried father may apply for a parental responsibility order under the Children Act, 1989.[2] The Government is proposing to make this automatic where the unmarried parents jointly register the birth.[3] Gay rights exponents want this extended to 'co-parents'. At the moment lesbian or homosexual 'partners' can only apply for a Joint Residence Order under the Children Act, 1989. This allows the 'partner' to be involved in decisions about the child's life, but responsibility is terminated at 16 and it does not establish inheritance or maintenance. Great hopes are invested in Article 8 of the European Convention on Human Rights (the right to privacy and family life).

The law in other countries

In the last decade, Denmark, Norway, Iceland and Sweden have legalised same-sex domestic partnerships, extending to registered partnerships virtually all the social and economic consequences of marriage. However, while all these countries have reputations as being 'progressive' in sexual and family matters, they are certainly not permissive when it comes to child rearing by same-sex couples. The suggestion is that adults are not free to do as they wish in regard to children, or to subject children to the effects of atypical adult sexual preferences. Icelandic law excludes same-sex couples from adoption and artificial insemination. In Denmark, same-sex couples may not in general adopt a child, but if one partner already has children their registered partner may adopt them. Swedish law excludes adoption, joint custody, and in vitro fertilisation for registered same-sex domestic partners. In Norway same-sex registered partnerships may not adopt.

Gay rights advances have been made elsewhere, however, under general discrimination statutes, which bypass considerations of child welfare. In Canada, the Family Law Act 1986's definition of spouse was modified to include same-sex couples. These same-sex couples cannot contract a marriage but their status has been made equivalent to a spouse in the 1986 Act. This followed a challenge under Section 15 of the Canadian Charter of Rights and Freedoms 1982, which prohibits discrimination on such grounds as race, ethnic origin, colour, religion, sex, age or mental or physical disability. The Supreme Court of Canada held that sexual orientation is also implicitly covered by the Charter. In light of this the Child and Family Services Act 1990 was also amended to permit same-sex joint adoption applications.

'Gay' marriage

Recognition for 'gay' marriage inevitably means that businesses would have to subsidise homosexual relationships, even if these are essentially non-generative. Children would be taught that homosexuality is equivalent in every way to heterosexual, marital relationships and, with sodomy a protected status, 'anti-discriminatory' legislation would be used against those who believe that marriage is between a man and a woman. Of course, the argument is that homosexuals should not be denied a whole range of protections and privileges available to married heterosexuals. At present, homosexuals, like any other citizens, can draft any Will they want, buy or rent homes with anyone they want, and the same goes for powers of attorney in cases of decrepitude. Gay rights advocates are themselves ambiguous about marriage, seeing equality either in terms of access to marriage or its abolition:

> "Lesbians, in particular, favour campaigns for full individualisation of social and economic rights, which would remove the legal consequences that flow from married status, so that rights and responsibilities would belong to individuals. Others want full access to the same couple rights as hetero-sexuals, including pension rights, inheritance, immigration etc, without necessarily having to formally register a partnership. The most controversial issue among interviewees, however, is related to the formal recognition of partnerships and the question of 'gay marriage', an issue which often divides couples. On the one hand, there is the desire for the same rights as heterosexuals. As a gay man says: 'I don't want partnership rights, I want marriage'. On the other hand, there is the discourse of difference. A lesbian states this forcefully: 'I just think it's a piece of nonsense, really...I believe now we are not the same as straight people...'"[4]

There is a certain distaste among gay activists for the idea that same-sex relationships may be accorded the status of family (with the entitlements attached to this), if this is at the price of behaving in a prescribed manner and replicating husband/wife relationships. At the same time it is not uncommon to hear naive claims that, if only homosexuals were allowed to marry and parent like heterosexuals, the more troubling aspects of 'gay' behaviour, like rampant promiscuity, would disappear, attributed as these are to social exclusion. Thus, following on from sentimental notions of stable couples yearning for lifetime commitments, is the belief that "if society gives its blessing to same-sex marriages gay couples would behave increasingly like straight couples. That is exactly what concerns many gays and lesbians".[5] Instead: "gays and lesbians should continue to develop their own culture, their own forms of association...imitating heterosexual marriage would constrain and destroy this creative and liberating effort."[6] Given this, the movement to 'gay marriage' is often fuelled more by a desire to transform and then destroy marriage itself, rather than to conform to its requirements. Faithfulness or fidelity is a particular target, with 'gay' male relationships seen to be superior to heterosexual married relationships because the 'need' for outside sex is recognised.

So far, 30 American states have resisted and banned homosexual marriage and Congress has passed the Defense of Marriage Act in 1996. Despite hopes to the contrary, in December 1999, the Hawaii High Court ruled against the effort of same-sex couples to have legal marriage. California and Vermont have instituted a same-sex partnership registration scheme which falls short of marriage.

Homosexuals as pioneers of family change

Seen as spearheading desirable family change, as part of a general sexual emancipation, homosexuals are said to be involved in families of choice, or 'elective families' or 'everyday experiments in living' involving 'fluid and adaptable networks' or 'social possibilities' which break with the 'constraints of traditional institutional patterns'. The 'chosen' family is "a powerful signifier, affirming the validity of homosexual ways of life". The belief is that "same-sex relationships offer unique possibilities for the construction of egalitarian relationships...non-heterosexuals have consciously shaped their relationships in opposition to assumed heterosexual models".[7] These are superior to heterosexual families, since they do not involve repressive and restrictive concepts like obligation or duties. Instead, "the decision to pursue a socially ostracized domain of intimacy" goes with a tendency to "embrace comparatively high standards of emotional intimacy and satisfaction".[8] According to Anthony Giddens, Tony Blair's guru of the 'third way', the increasing separation of sexuality from reproduction (and reproduction from sexuality by technological developments), has put it outside of all institutional and moral control and made it simply a vehicle for self-expression and self-actualisation.[9] Such 'plastic (sic) sexuality' is part of the 'project of self' and realised in 'pure relationships', which are sustained from within themselves: not supported by, anchored in, regulated or constrained by any social standards, laws, conventions or rules. Entered into for their own sake, what "...holds the pure relationship together is the acceptance on the part of each partner, 'until further notice', that each gains sufficient benefit from the relation to make its continuance worthwhile."[10] Such a 'transformation of intimacy' as Giddens sees happening is a fulfilment of the dreams of Herbert Marcuse and Wilhelm Reich for complete sexual emancipation. The difference is that these sexual radicals who inspired the 1960s counterculture, saw a version of the Marxist revolution, or overthrow of capitalism by socialism, as the essential prerequisite. In contrast, Giddens sees the "advancement of self-autonomy in the context of pure relationships" or "the democratising of personal life" going hand in hand with the development of democracy in the wider community and even "in the global political order at the most extensive level."[11] However, while "...marriage 'in the traditional sense' is disappearing, it is the gays who are the pioneers in this respect – the prime everyday experimenters".[12]

It is argued that law and public policy, which previously supported marriage, must intervene to prevent support for marriage, or eradicate bias or 'discrimination on the basis of marital status'. This would be achieved by creating a single statutory regime governing couple relationships, whatever the sexual orientation, or by abolishing all benefits or distinctions based on 'family' and marital status. Either would, it is argued, blend social justice and compassion with the goal of personal freedom, by creating a level playing field for all relationships – entirely non-prescriptive as well as non-discriminatory. Either would complete the casualisation of changing, serial relationships – in line with the development and demands of plastic sexuality and expressive individualism.

There is a problem with the place of children in this world of ad hoc, fluid relationships. A dominant idea, favoured by many politicians, pundits and policy makers, is to separate contractual commitment to a child from marriage, with unmarried and married fathers having the same rights and the same obligations, grounded in the 'fact of parenthood'. People would move in and out of sexual or other relationships, but somehow continue to 'parent' children in the same or different households. This would accommodate homosexual parents.

Human rights and wrongs

Advocacy of same-sex parenting utilises two kinds of arguments. One is based on human rights, where classification based on gender is discriminatory.

"The time has now come for the present Government to reform the law of adoption in this country and to permit any couple who demonstrate their suitability as parents to adopt jointly as a couple, irrespective of status or sexual orientation. The reasons for this are threefold...

First, under a reformulated family values ideology, what is important is a couple's commitment to successful parenting, not their status or sexual orientation. Secondly, the objective of the law in this context is to secure the best arrangement for the child's future welfare, and this should be assessed free from biased and unjustified assumptions about the capacity of certain family forms to promote a child's welfare. Thirdly, an argument can be made under the Human Rights Act 1998 that the current law on adoption is incompatible with equal access by unmarried couples to the right to respect for family life which is protected by Art 8."[13]

Insofar as present law gives preference to heterosexual adults over homosexual adults in parental relationships, it is seen as unjust, as it is when it discriminates between married and unmarried parents. This amounts to more than a matter of simply tolerating 'diversity', since human history, anthropology and, above all, biology, provide us with no precedents for a 'family' with two men or two women at its nucleus. To avoid discrimination, the law must now undo handicaps present in nature, as well as those of social origin, although it is disputed whether procreative hetero-sex is "more 'natural' than homosexual acts or bisexuality. Heterosexuality simply has the weight of ideological and material privilege behind it"[14] which can be undone. Even so, it still happens to be an inescapable 'fact of nature' that only two people, not three or fifty, and only a man and a woman, not two men or four women, nor a woman and a gerbil, can make a child. But, not withstanding that people of the same-sex cannot have children by normal reproductive processes, "gay couples are entitled to the same fundamental procreative freedoms as heterosexual couples."[15] Thus, the Stonewall lecturer would delete from section 13 (5) of the Human Fertilisation and Embryology Act 1990 the reference to a child's need for a father "which to my mind smacks too much of unreconstructed family values ideology". Furthermore: "An equality question for the future must be access by gay men to surrogacy" where, under the present law, "only a married commissioning couple may apply for a parental order in respect of a child born through a surrogacy arrangement".[16]

Such argument about a 'right to adopt' or 'procreative rights' involves an adult agenda which is independent of claims about the welfare or needs of children. The debate is not about recognizing individual exceptions or legitimising homosexual parenting on a case-by-case basis in special or individual cases. It is not just about abolishing procedures which prevent appropriate people from being able to adopt because of group membership, but about all individuals in certain groups having the 'right to adopt'. Instead of finding the most appropriate family for the child, agencies would have to ensure that people have an adopted (or surrogate) child. It is not about having two parents, even a same-sex couple, because two parents are better than one or none, or how parenting by an adult who is engaged in homosexual relationships might be the best option for a particular child or children. Such an argument recognises, for example, the failures of alternatives to parenting (like institutional care or impermanent fostering), and that few, if any, parenting situations are perfect.

Values must be fact

Rights arguments are usually backed up by sociological or empirical claims – that same-sex parents can provide parenting that is just as good and valuable for children (in terms of outcomes) as that provided by heterosexual married couples. This makes it arbitrary and irrational that "[l]esbians have been refused access to donor insemination and permission to adopt or foster children on the grounds that they would be less able than heterosexual parents to provide an optimal family environment."[17]

Advocates for legalisation of homosexual parenting seek to establish a general rule that homosexual relations must be and are fully equal, or just as good as and equivalent in all ways, to heterosexual parenting. This calls for a finding of scientific, as well as normative, fact. Thus, the Stonewall lecturer insists that "family values ideology and discourse...must be reformulated to meet the demands of diversity in a pluralist society"[18] and attacks "highly questionable assumptions...that certain family forms are inherently more capable of promoting the interests of children and adults than others ...[and therefore] that certain family forms are morally more deserving than others".[19] Attempts have already been made to equate childrearing by one-parent or reconstituted families with that of the original married parents. Now 'gay' and lesbian parents – as much or more – are seen as being at the cutting edge of the emerging, exciting multiplicity of 'new family forms'. Indeed, such is 'gay creativity', that "beyond the confines of heterosexuality, women are finding all sorts of creative ways to parent, and to collaborate successfully with gay men...".[20] If the development of children born into lesbian mother homes is demonstrably normal, then this challenges the need for fathers, and questions whether a male and female parent are at all necessary or desirable for children's development. It achieves and fully vindicates the 'father free' society, so that the end of patriarchy is in sight. As the wish must be the reality, it is predicted that children "who derive their principal source of love, discipline, protection and identification from women living independent of male domestic authority or influence should develop less stereotypical symbolic, emotional, practical, and behavioural gender repertoires."[21]

The Scottish Court of Session, in making an adoption order in favour of a gay man living with a 'partner', emphasized not only that the capacity of a particular couple to promote an individual child's welfare should be assessed without 'stereotyped preconceptions', but that 'judicial notice' was taken "of the absence of evidence (as opposed to preconception) that homosexual relationships are less stable or caring than heterosexual relationships, or that children in a homosexual family are more likely themselves to be homosexual, or that they will be stigmatised in their social relations."[22]

Historical inevitability

Claims from both rights and evidence have a tendency to be swept up in an argument from historical inevitability. Here, an 'is', or a 'will be', slips into an 'ought'. We find that standards are being read off from the direction of trends, which we are bidden to accommodate, and affirm, just because they are happening. Thus, changing social conditions should of necessity bring about legal and other changes, because change is taken to vindicate itself and possesses a moral authority of its own. Around 70 per cent of children still live in a married household.[23] But since this group is not increasing proportionally, and it is the 'direction of future norms' that counts, we are repeatedly told how a "policy framework that responds to the current realities of family life"[sic] is one "which recognises that increasingly children will be brought up in 'non-traditional' family forms,"[24] which will include same-sex couples. Often the future is now, with claims that the "nuclear family of heterosexual mother and father raising one or more of their own biological children is no longer the norm…".[25] This suggests that these are oddities or throwbacks which are already outnumbered by homosexuals raising non-biological children. The latter are treated with tremendous deference and significance, while we are meant to mock with the spokesperson from the British Agencies for Adoption and Fostering "that the tabloids' idea of a family comprises two parents of different sexes,"[26] as if these were a rare occurrence, or an insignificant or unusual minority. Nobody has to accept the morality of the future simply because it is the behaviour of the future, even if it were unalterable. By itself, neither the extent nor demographic prevalence of lone, married or homosexual parents tells us what is best in terms of any particular outcome. If smoking or grapefruit eating was increasing, would this make either one worthy of promotion or endorsement, let alone good for health?

Assessing the evidence

The empirical debate and evaluation of evidence on the outcomes of different 'family forms' involves considerations of overall outcomes for children and society in general. This means comparisons of the general childrearing abilities of heterosexual and homosexual couples or individuals as classes or groups. This recognises that no particular parenting situation is inevitably going to be associated with poor or good outcomes considered on a case by case basis. Some children may be doing better in an 'alternative' family situation than others in a two-parent heterosexual family – or a child may be doing worse in a traditional conjugal household compared to others with lesbians. In turn, neither the degree to which the traditional or conjugal family is acclaimed or execrated, alters the *fact* that family structures may differ in the opportunities they extend to growing children.

Actually it is irrelevant what a reviewer or critic's views are on a particular subject – in this instance, same-sex parenting or homosexuality. What is important, is the veracity or validity of the observations or objections that are made – not where they come from. But whether or not homosexual parenting is actually better or, at least much the same, for children compared to heterosexual parenting is an explosive subject.

Indeed, it is one of the most controversial and emotion laden issues in human development that anyone can deal with. The tendency is for most extravagant claims about its benefits to be taken at face value, out of respect and support for homosexuals, while any critical evaluation or examination of the work to hand is apt to invoke furious reflex accusations about homophobia. Expressing any doubts results in righteous attacks about personal insults to endearing 'lesbigays'. It is not the only area where it is insisted that fact and value must coincide. Other prominent examples are childcare, working mothers and lone-parenting and increasingly, unmarried and divorced fathers. The result is that "Some findings, and the methods and analyses that discern them, are simply more 'politically correct' than others. For science, this is a major problem".[27] There is fear for professional and academic reputations, where the promotion, tenures and research funds of those who speak out are at risk. Academics and researchers tend to cowardice anyway, something reinforced by an ivory tower snobbery against involvement in 'vulgar' public debate. A mention in the *Daily Mail* is considered a fate worse than death, even if the reportage is entirely accurate.

What must be borne in mind when considering claims about homosexual parenting, is that no amount of decrying or demonstrating the disadvantages of one situation is, in itself, proof of the advantages of another. Deficiencies or condemnations of heterosexual parenting are not, in themselves, valid evidence for the superiority of homosexual parenting. For example: the Children's Society agrees "with the many people who have written to us to say that the ideal setting for children is with a mother and father who are married and committed to one another. That is also our ideal." Nevertheless: "the children who need foster or adoptive families have been failed by that ideal and many have experienced trauma and abuse in their families."[28] However, it is difficult to see how children are being 'failed' by the ideal of 'a mother and father who are married and committed to each other', or how anyone can be failed by an 'ideal' come to that. Are the robbed 'failed' by the idea of honesty?

But how much in reality are children 'failed' by 'a mother and father who are married'? As it is, three out of four children entering the English care system are not living with both parents.[29] Indeed, the "most striking feature of all" about the backgrounds of children going into care, is the way these "magnify...accelerating social trends in a most vivid and exaggerated way" in the degree to which their families are "incomplete, disrupted, or restructured following earlier breakdowns".[30] Children are particularly likely to go into care following a crisis when a family is being 'reconstituted'.

How many and who?

Who are we talking about, or how prevalent are homosexual parents, and how many homosexuals have children? The 1996 General Household Survey estimated that only 0.1 per cent of households in Great Britain were headed by a same-sex couple.[31] The Labour Force Survey of autumn 1999 estimated that 0.2 per cent of households were headed by a same-sex couple.[32] An extensive, self administered questionnaire on sexual issues was given to 10,115 adults during random sampling in six US cities in 1983 and 1984, yielding a response rate of around a half (but 85 per cent of those aged 35 or under).[33] About seven per cent of gays and about a third of lesbians were parents, but less than 1 per cent of parents generally were either bisexual or homosexual. It was estimated that, in the US as a whole, perhaps 0.15 per cent to 0.5 per cent of children have a homosexual parent. Around 60 per cent of heterosexual males had at least one child, compared to around 50 per cent of those deeming themselves bisexual and 6.3 per cent of homosexual males. The proportions for females were over 70 per cent; 36.5 per cent and nearly 27 per cent respectively. Other estimates, from more sympathetic sources, give the number of US children aged 19 and under with lesbian or gay parents as between one and 12 per cent of all children. However, the latter figure depends upon classifying as a lesbian or gay parent anyone to whom the idea of homoerotic love has ever been appealing and the former on self-identification as lesbian or gay.[34]

The majority of children of homosexuals are born in the context of a heterosexual relationship. This includes those where the parents divorce when the husband 'comes out' as gay or the wife as a lesbian; families which divorce when both the husband and wife come out as gay or lesbian, and families in which one of, or both, the husband and wife come out and they decide not to divorce. "The gay or lesbian parent may be either the residential or the non-residential parent, or children may live part of the time in both homes".[35] Gay or lesbian parents may be single, or they may have same-sex partners, and the gay or lesbian partner may or may not take up a step-parenting relationship with the children. If both same-sex partners bring children with them, the youngsters may also be cast into step-sibling relationships with one another.

In addition to children born in the context of heterosexual relationships, both single and coupled lesbians are increasingly giving birth to children. The majority are believed to be conceived through donor insemination (DI), with unknown or known sperm donors (who might be a friend, relative, or acquaintance). When sperm donors are known, they may or may not take parental, avuncular, or other roles in respect of the children who are born using donor insemination. Options pursued by gay men seeking parenthood include adoption and fostering of [unrelated] children. "Through DI or sexual intercourse, gay men may also become biological fathers of children whom they intend to co-parent with a single woman (whether lesbian or heterosexual), with a lesbian couple, or with another gay male..."[36]

There are predictions that, as homosexuality becomes 'normalised' or more legitimate, the numbers of children with homosexual parents procreated within marriage may fall, since fewer people will feel compelled to conceal or thwart their homosexual inclinations in this way. This assumption leans upon questionable notions of early 'fixed' sexuality. People who later identify as homosexual may have married, not to 'escape' homophobia, but because they saw themselves as heterosexual earlier in life. Even if these predictions are correct, this will probably only decrease the number of homosexual men who become parents, although there are more homosexual men than lesbian women. [37] The proportion of lesbian parents may not change much and may even increase, as it becomes increasingly acceptable for single women to have children. Men alone, of whatever sexual persuasion, less frequently desire children and, if they do, have fewer means of acquiring them.

Endnotes:

1 Editorial Essay in *Lesbian and Gay Fostering and Adoption- Extraordinary Yet Ordinary*, Hicks, S and McDermott, J (Eds.), Jessica Kingsley Publications, London, 1999, page 147

2 Children Act 1989 Section 4(1)

3 Adoption and Children Bill 2001 Clause 106

4 Weeks J, Donovan, C and Heaphy, B, *Families of Choice: The Structure and Meanings of Non-Heterosexual Relationships*, Research Results, No 6, Economic and Social Research Council, 1997

5 Hartman, A, 'The Long Road to Equality: Lesbians and Social Policy', in Laird J (Ed.) *Lesbians and Lesbian Families*, Columbia University Press, New York, 1999, page 113

6 *Ibid*, page 112

7 Weeks J, Donovan, C and Heaphy, B, *Op cit*

8 Stacey, J and Biblarz, T J, '(How) does the Sexual Orientation of Parents Matter?', *American Sociological Review*, 66, 2001, page 177

9 Giddens, A, *The Transformation of Intimacy,* Polity Press, 1992, page 27
   See also Hall, D R, 'Marriage as a Pure Relationship: Exploring the Link Between Premarital Cohabitation and Divorce in Canada', *Journal of Comparative Family Studies*, 27 (1), Spring 1996, pages 1-12

10 Giddens, A, *Op cit*, page 63

11 *Ibid*, pages 195-196

12 *Ibid*, page 135

13 Bailey-Harris, R, 'Third Stonewall Lecture – Lesbian and Gay Family Values and the Law', *Family Law,* Aug 1999, page 565

14 Ryan, A, 'From Moralism to Sexual Democracy', in Jesson B, Ryan, A and Spoonley, P (Eds.) *Revival of the Right- New Zealand Politics in the 1980s*, Heinemann Reed, Auckland, 1988, page 121

15 Barrie Drewitt and Tony Barlow quoted in Steyn, M, 'Fatherhood is Fine, But this is Ridiculous', *The Sunday Telegraph*, 31 October 1999

16 Bailey-Harris, R, *Op cit*, page 566

17 Tasker, F and Golombok, S, 'Adults Raised as Children in Lesbian Families', *American Journal of Orthopsychiatry* 65(2), 1995, page 203

18 Bailey-Harris, R, *Op cit*, page 560

19 *Loc cit*

20 Dunne, G, 'Lesbians make better parents', *Stonewall* 8 (1), July, 1999, page 14

21   Stacey, J and Biblarz, T J, *Op cit*, page 177
22   Singer, J, in *Re W (Adoption: Homosexual Adopter)* [1997] 2FLR 406. Quoted in Bailey-Harris R, *Op cit*, page 565
23   House of Commons, Hansard, 11 May 2001, col. 435 wa
24   Buchanan, A and Brinke, J T, *What Happened When They Were Grown Up?*, Joseph Rowntree Foundation, 1997, page x
25   Lott-Whitehead, L and Tully, C T, 'The Family Lives of Lesbian Mothers', in Laird J (Ed.) *Lesbians and Lesbian Families*, Columbia University Press, New York, 1999, page 243
26   Chambers, L, 'Gay adopters' The Magistrates Debate, *The Magistrate*, February 2000
27   Belsky, J and Eggebeen, D 'Scientific Criticism and the Study of Early and Extensive Maternal Employment', *Journal of Marriage and the Family*, 53, 1991, page 1108
28   The Children's Society, *Information on the Children's Society Change of Policy on Adoption and Fostering*, August 1999, page 3
29   Bebbington, A and Miles, J, 'The Background of Children who enter Local Authority Care', *British Journal of Social Work*, 19, 1989, page 353
30   Packman J, Randall, J and Jacques, N, *Who Needs Care? Social-Work decisions about Children,* Basil Blackwell, 1986, pages 32, 34
31   House of Commons, Hansard, 11 November 1997, col. 507 wa
32   House of Commons, Hansard, 11 May 2000, col. 471 wa (Cohabiting with same-sex refers to same sex couples and not siblings or platonic friends)
33   Cameron, P and Cameron, K, 'Homosexual Parents', *Adolescence* 31(124), Winter 1996, pages 757-776
34   Stacey, J and Biblarz, T J, *Op cit*, pages 164-165
35   Patterson, C J, 'Children of Lesbian and Gay Parents', *Child Development* 63, 1992, page 1027
36   *Loc cit*
37   Stacey, J and Biblarz, T J, *Op cit*, page 165

Chapter 2
How good is the evidence?

In the last analysis, research questions (and findings) as to whether or not there are differences between children reared by heterosexual and same-sex parents are essentially distinct from the evaluations of whether any discovered or discoverable outcomes are socially and morally desirable or not. However, questions about outcomes for children of gay and lesbian parents often relate to fears about adjustment, sexual orientation, abuse, social isolation and problems with peers.

The leading questions

1. Will children growing up with homosexual parents be psychologically less healthy than those growing up with two heterosexual parents, or will they be more or less vulnerable to mental breakdown, adjustment or behaviour problems, or difficulties with social relationships?

2. Will children growing up with homosexual parents themselves be more likely to be lesbian and gay? Until recently, 'expert' as much as common opinion was that homosexuality, like drug use, was a learned pathology, passed on by modelling and seduction, so that the children of homosexuals might be more inclined to acquire parental sexual proclivities,[1] just as they would be more inclined to be church goers or smokers or drinkers if their parents were religious, smokers or drinkers, and so forth.[2] Yet,

coexisting with claims that sexual orientation is fixed, if not by birth, then from very early on in life, are notions about individuals being free to 'choose' from 'diverse lifestyles' and fluid 'sexualities'. According to the Children's Society, the

> "research evidence is that homosexual childcare has very marginal impact on adult sexuality...Whilst there are probably many causes of homosexual orientation in adulthood, most research suggests that a person's sexuality is heavily influenced by relationships (or absence of relationships) with parents and close family in early childhood...over the age of 8, the sexuality of adult carers is likely to have little impact".[3]

3. Will the homosexuals' liaisons and activities result in an increased likelihood of children being neglected, subjected to much conflict and upheaval or even abused – increasing the probability of various forms of sexual victimisation from the parents' associates, if not the parents themselves?

4. Will the children reared by homosexuals be more likely to be teased, ridiculed, ostracised, or otherwise bullied and rejected by peers? Will they have a less happy or more miserable time on average because their unusual circumstances cause them to be socially isolated? Poor peer relationships are generally a risk factor in development. Anyway, is it not cruel to place children with lesbian or gay couples, if they may commonly fear that they, too, will be gay or that people will think they are gay?

The confident answers

All these fears tend to be dismissed as "...myths, and their effect on public policy, frustrates the attempts of many gay and lesbian persons who seek to adopt as single parents".[4] The "belief that a child raised in a household with a lesbian or gay parent is more likely to become lesbian or gay is without any basis in fact".[5] In turn, there is "no...evidence that even suggests that lesbian and gay parents are more likely to sexually abuse their children, or to allow them to be molested by others".[6]

Recent professional literature and opinion stresses either the irrelevance or advantage of parental homosexuality for child rearing. Some, such as the Children's Society charity even suggest that superior homosexual parents can rescue the fall out, or repair the damage, caused by the pathological nuclear family. As part of its strong support for the gay rights movement, the American Psychological Association, for example, insists that homosexuals are as fully effective parents as heterosexuals. Purportedly: "not a single study has found children of gay or lesbian parents to be disadvantaged in any significant respect relative to children of heterosexual parents".[7] Indeed, homosexual parenting is said to "raise the possibility of various desirable outcomes for these children. For instance, won't these children grow up with increased tolerance for viewpoints other than their own? Won't they be more at home in the multicultural environments that Americans increasingly inhabit?"[8] At a public debate in London attended by the present author in early 2000, a psychologist denounced as "meaningless authoritarianism" any idea that two married parents are in any way better than other "family forms", while claiming that "people of the same sex are experts in parenting", or the "most thoughtful parents in the country today." Statements suggesting that homosexual parents provide superior child rearing are now common. For example:

> "...the results indicate that families of lesbian mothers have numerous strengths – strengths sometimes lacking in more traditional families. The strengths include an open climate for sexuality, a healthy respect for difference, including, but not limited to sexual orientation, and an accepting, nurturing environment conducive to human growth."[9]

This all suggests that the research on this issue is "so rigorous, compelling, and definitive that it enables a prudent person or a professional association to completely disregard common or traditional opinion."[10] Indeed, the

"...certitude of...professional associations on these points is astounding. Social science is usually incapable of answering any question definitively".[11] While intact marriage might be regarded as "the gold standard for child rearing", we are being told that "there is an exception to this standard" provided by another child rearing environment that of homosexual parents.[12]

As it is, there is now a massive body of evidence suggesting that children who grow up with both original parents tend, on the whole, to be better off than children living with single parents and in step-families, in terms of all or most outcomes. Even studies endeavouring to control for a host of other factors, which minimise the absence of one parent, cannot make the effects of family structure disappear, or make the results go in the opposite direction.[13] Compared to being reared by single or cohabiting parents, relatives, foster parents or in institutions, children born or adopted and raised in an intact marriage are more apt to avoid legal and psychiatric trouble, become well educated, be gainfully employed, and in turn to get and stay married and raise the next generation. The U.K. National Child Development Study, explores the relationships between children's parenting experiences and what happens in adult life. There is a gradient of risk, where children brought up by both birth parents had the lowest risk for psychological problems at every age, followed by restructured families, and lone-parents.[14] Whether or not adverse economic circumstances lead to the formation of lone-parent households, conditions are created in which children are *more vulnerable all the time*.[15] Parallel data from the 1988 National Health Interview Survey on Child Health, involving 17,110 US children aged 17 or under, found that of behaviour problems, anti-social behaviour, anxiety and depression, headstrong behaviour, hyperactivity, dependency, peer conflict and social withdrawal were higher at lower income levels, and then tended to diminish up the income scale for children in all circumstances. However, within all income bands the differences between children from different family types persist.[16]

Heterosexuals – the real child abusers?

The Children's Society believes that children are safer with homosexuals, since the "vast majority of child abuse is committed by heterosexuals, within the context of an ordinary family with married or cohabiting parents."[17] This has long been demonstrable as nonsense and there is no excuse for a leading children's charity to reiterate what has never been more than anti-family rhetoric.

Children from backgrounds of family disruption comprise a majority of the victims of all major forms of active child abuse, physical, emotional and sexual, and a majority of victims of neglect, despite being greatly outnumbered in the population by children from intact two-parent homes.[18] Paternal absenteeism is often combined with the presence of unrelated males in households with children. In reality as in folklore: "The presence of a step-parent is the best epidemiological predictor of child abuse risk yet discovered". This runs the gamut from sexual molestation to fatal battering, and is statistically independent of poverty, maternal age and family size.[19] The risk from a man without either a blood or legal tie to the children in the household (i.e. the boyfriend) is greatest of all.[20] Fragmented families also afford poorer protection from opportunistic males in the surrounding community, and account for the vast majority of non-parental child abuse.[21] This may be a factor in the earlier sexual activity and pregnancy rates of girls of lone-mothers, since many young teens report being coerced by older boys.[22]

Uncomfortable and ideologically inappropriate though it may be, the evidence is that around a third of all molestations of children are homosexual molestations, and the same applies to the proportion of paedophiles who are homosexual.[23] It is thoroughly misleading to state how "it must be repeated that most paedophiles are heterosexual men" without taking into account the relative proportions of homosexuals and heterosexuals in the population.[24] Project SIGMA found that 20 per cent of the 'gay' men in their study first had sex with a man who was 10 or more years older.[25] In turn, nearly a quarter (24 per cent) of the men had been raped or coerced into sexual activity by another man,[26] and homosexual rapes are over-represented in the UK crime figures.[27] The horrendous catalogue of abuse of children in institutions which has been brought to light in recent years has been overwhelmingly perpetrated by men on boys. The Waterhouse report on events in North Wales said that the Tribunal of Inquiry had heard evidence claiming that the Chester branch of the Campaign for Homosexual Equality had been used as a means of 'picking up' under-aged boys.[28] Many of the individuals mentioned in this and other investigations are serving sentences for buggering and indecently assaulting boys. Political correctness has played a part in hampering the exposure of abusers, or even helped these get access to children, given that people are afraid of being accused of homophobia, or want to appear 'right-on'.[29]

The status of the evidence

At the very least with the promotion of homosexual parenting, there is often a presumption of 'no harm', so that the burden of proof is made to fall on those who are unhappy about the idea. However, as a radical social and moral change is being proposed, the burden of proof should fall on those who *want* the change.[30] In turn, while the authors of studies have every right to advocate adoption, fertility and 'partnership' rights for same-sex individuals and couples, so do others to voice their disagreement:

> "…the stakes in obtaining valid answers to these research questions are very high. It is not enough for a study to be interesting, or raise important questions about a subject, or to be provocative. While these criteria may be enough to get a study published, they are not strong enough to justify dramatic alterations in long-established public policies. To justify changes…studies should be strong enough that policy makers have faith in the study's reliability, and confidence that more research is unlikely to overturn its findings.

This is not an unreasonable requirement. The public policy consequences of relying on inadequate or insufficient studies can be devastating."[31]

We have had proclamations from 'experts' that divorce was a costless exercise for children who, if anything, had all to gain from a 'second chance'; that growing up with a lone-parent had no negative consequences that could not be explained in terms of economics, and that marriage was a threat to women's mental health and economic advancement. Although acted upon and still endlessly repeated, often by people who ought to know better, these assumptions have been overthrown by more rigorous research. There is a duty to examine the veracity of studies cited to back proposals that may have a dramatic impact upon children and society, rather than look away so as not to offend the sensibilities of activists.

Rather than the research into homosexual parenting being "an island of certitude", in what is "often a turbulent sea of conflicting claims based upon inconsistent data", the main problem is that there is so little that allows us to make any meaningful comparisons.[32] The only definite outcome of the research is the overwhelmingly one-sided position being taken in social science literature in support of homosexual parenting. Instead of any and every one conclusively proving that children raised by homosexuals are no different from children raised by heterosexuals, two academic reviewers conclude: "that the methods used...are so flawed that these studies prove nothing. Therefore, they should not be used in legal cases to make any arguments about 'homosexual vs. heterosexual' parenting. Their claims have no basis."[33] Failure to design the study properly, failure to properly measure the relevant variables, failure to control for extraneous variables, and failure to use the proper statistical tests invalidates a study. If a study claims to find no difference i.e.:

"Non-significant results", and "failed to carry out one or more of these research links in the proper manner, its conclusions are purely and simply invalid. Why? Because failing to carry out correctly one or more of these essential elements, in and of itself increases the chances of finding non-significant results. In other words, if you look for wrong findings using wrong methods, it is even more likely you'll get wrong results."[34]

Anecdotal 'studies'

Many 'studies' of same-sex parenting are little more than anecdotal. Indeed, gushing personal testimonies are often the foremost 'evidence' used to vindicate homosexual parenting as being as good or better than anything heterosexuals can provide. While anecdotes may illustrate conclusions drawn from well-conducted research, in themselves they prove nothing. Confirming instances, or 'facts', or cases, can be found to be consistent with any viewpoint or theory that has, or could, be proposed, including alien landings, food-free diets, and any magical or 'miracle' cure. If anything, anecdotal 'evidence' which runs contrary to a claim is more useful. Such potentially falsifying observations are a crucial test of a proposed law or theory, and suggest that this is invalid – or, at least in its original form, needs modifying. Moreover, it must be remembered that anecdotes are unlikely to represent the full record, but are usually presentations of 'edited' versions of events. Bearing these observations in mind, consider the 'case' of Cherie Taylor, in a lesbian relationship in New Zealand in the early '80s. The couple went public with their three children and presented themselves in the media as an example of a normal and near perfect family.

"However, in the early '90s Cherie separated from her partner. She now felt she and her partner had deliberately misled the New Zealand public, and sought to repair the damage through publicity. Suitable 'penitent' material was published in papers (Rorani, 1994; Taylor, 1994). Among other things, she said the level of violence between her and her partner had been high, and that the children were not happy about the overall arrangement. She had not previously told the media that one of the boys had been in counselling for anger management for years; he was particularly incensed that he could not be told who his father was (the father was heterosexually married).

Cherie was under immense pressure from the gay/lesbian community to rejoin their ranks and eventually did so. In 1998 she sued her ex-partner for child maintenance, and won."[35]

Similarly, in the UK a couple of lesbians each had a child by using sperm from male friends stored in a pickle jar, after being refused NHS fertility treatment. In 1996, one had said how "Some children are in an environment where the parents split up and this is not good for the child. This is not going to be the case with us. We have a loving, solid relationship." They had a 'gay marriage' conducted by a female vicar in a pub. In 1999, the other revealed, "We are both going our separate ways because we do not love each other any more."[36]

It is astonishing how collections of anecdotes are reverentially accepted by public bodies, academics and research institutes, who would immediately laugh away the use of similar material as 'evidence' elsewhere. The ideological bias in favour of homosexuality and gay rights and against the conjugal family results in an immense double standard. A briefing paper produced for an adoption conference (at which this author was present) by The Family Policy Studies Centre cites, as a "study of gay men and women who had fostered or adopted children", just such a collection of self-congratulatory testimonials to show that homosexuals are as successful as anyone else in this area and "an under-used resource who could meet the needs of particular children."[37] Its reception should be contrasted with that given shortly afterwards to the presenter of the findings from the large scale US longitudinal Study of Marital Stability over the Life Course.[38] Conclusions that low conflict marriages ending in divorce meant poorer outcomes for children and that most marriages that now ended in divorce were low conflict marriages were clearly unwelcome. Despite the study's meticulous attention to a multitude of variables, an audience clearly hostile to any notion that divorce harms or that marriage might be at all beneficial for children, subjected it to the most detailed scrutiny, as they scrabbled around trying to find alternative explanations for the findings or fault with the sample.

If anecdotes may be used to promote adoption by homosexuals, then – contrariwise – anecdote is that Wayne Tardiff and his partner, Allan Yoder, had been the first homosexual couple permitted to become adoptive parents (of a three-year-old boy) in New Jersey. Yoder died of AIDS a few months later and the child had to be placed elsewhere.[39] Artie Wallace, a homosexual with AIDS, won a child-custody battle with his wife in 1988. Californian court-appointed experts recommended that he have sole custody of his ten-year-old son, in part because the mother had fled the state to keep the boy from being exposed to HIV. Artie Wallace died seven months later.[40] One of the first single men to adopt children in Florida, David Lindsey, got a 15 year prison term for homosexually abusing three of his 11 adopted sons.[41]

No hypothesis

Not far removed from the anecdotal are studies which simply 'explore the differences' between parents or their children, or 'examine the factors', or 'the family relationships and development of children'. Aims to 'look at' or 'describe the characteristics' of populations do not suffice as hypotheses for research purposes. (Two different family structures could be associated with different levels of crime, for example. But, even if the crime rate of one family structure was say 15 to 30 per cent higher than that of the other, crime still would not be 'characteristic' of any background, so connections would go unrecognised. Thus we would not know that it was family structure and not one of many other differences between the two groups that is related to the differences in crime rates.) A proper research hypothesis postulates some kind of causal mechanism operating in the world, where something, an independent variable, is stated to 'cause' something else, a dependent variable. This possible connection or relationship may, or may not be, confirmed. A majority, or 29, of the 49 original research studies on same-sex parenting reviewed by Robert Lerner and Althea Nagai in 2001, failed to produce a testable hypothesis.[42]

Testing the wrong hypothesis

Another 18 of the studies reviewed by Lerner and Nagai tried to affirm a null hypothesis, or explicitly sought to find no differences between heterosexual and same-sex parents in child outcomes. Starting with the expectation of finding no difference creates methodological problems 'unrecognised' by the authors: indeed, it "results in an undue partiality in interpreting their research findings and in carrying out the research itself."[43] This is because failure to reject the null hypothesis necessarily leads to an indeterminate result, since one cannot validly 'confirm' nothing, or a lack of any connection or effect. Thus, inverting the normal hypothesis testing situation makes it too easy to find for the null hypothesis "which is the outcome favoured by these researchers"[44], who may "falsely conclude that there is no difference between homosexual and heterosexual parents in child outcomes."[45] Moreover, conventional statistical procedures, developed for affirming a research hypothesis, are unsuitable when trying to find 'no difference'.

When a researcher investigates a posited relationship between two variables, the evidence may mean that they have to accept the research hypothesis, or that a difference between groups does exist and is not due to chance factors. The researcher will then see if the hypothesis can stand up to other tests of its validity. But if the investigation fails to confirm the research hypothesis (and so fails to reject a null hypothesis), this is not the same as 'proving' nothing or that no effect exists. It is possible that the sample may have been too small to reach a level of statistical significance; the significance level used may have been set too high, or the ways of measuring the independent and dependent variables might be so unreliable that no stable results are possible. Unfortunately:

> "If the investigator starts with the goal of finding no differences...without taking into account all these other aspects of a study that may go wrong...each poorly executed research step, such as setting up comparison groups, sampling, measurement, and statistical analysis, increases the likelihood of finding no difference." The "poorer research you do, the more successful you will be."[46]

No control: part 1

In testing a hypothesis, researchers have to impose controls on the research design to eliminate false answers, or use comparison groups, control for extraneous and suppressor variables, use pair or group matching and use multivariate statistical tests. Only one of the 49 studies listed by Robert Lerner and Althea Nagai used all five control methods, while 18 used no controls at all.[47] In a previous 1993 review, Philip A. Belcastro[48] and colleagues examined the methodological validity and reliability of 14 post 1975 studies addressing the effects of homosexual parenting on children's sexual and social functioning. They found that: "The most impressive finding is that all of the studies lacked external validity. Furthermore, not a single study remotely represented any sub-population of homosexual parents". Three studies met minimal to higher standards of internal validity, while the remaining eleven presented moderate to fatal threats to internal validity. The conclusion that "there are no significant differences in children reared by homosexual parents versus heterosexual parents is not supported by the published research base".[49]

An aside:'ghost data' and the reappearing studies

Philip A. Belcastro and colleagues could make no meta-analysis or collective statistical analysis due to inadequate data. Yet, it has been claimed that 'aggregated' studies show there is: "no data to suggest that children who have gay or lesbian parents are different in any aspects of psychological, social and sexual development from children in heterosexual families".[50] But combining any number of badly flawed studies is hardly going to produce a super one that is less flawed.

This is not the only citation of 'ghost data'. Versions of the same paper are apt to be recycled through the journals in such a way as to suggest that they represent separate studies or new work. Favourable reviews or commentaries on other work are referred to as if they were themselves original research projects, as are fawning magazine articles. According to Fiona Tasker and Susan Golombok, Charlotte J. Patterson shows how "children...born to, or adopted by, lesbian mothers were not found to differ from children of heterosexual parents on measures of social competence, behaviour problems, gender-role behaviour, or the extent to which they saw themselves as aggressive, sociable, or likely to enjoy being the centre of attention."[51] They omit to tell us that they are referring to her overview of other studies.

No control: part 2

Bias influences the research design and analyses as well as the data gathered. Seven studies surveyed by Belcastro did not use a control group – yet, at the absolute minimum, a study of whether parental sexual identities affect child outcomes needs a study group and a control group.[52] Of the 49 studies reviewed by Robert Lerner and Althea Nagai, 21 (or 43 per cent) had no heterosexual comparison group, making them scientifically useless and their conclusions invalid.[53] However, this does not prevent such studies being used for public policy pronouncements, as when investigators conclude how lesbian relationships can provide a valid relationship for child rearing on the basis of the greater relationship satisfaction of lesbian couples with children compared to those without, despite the work having no heterosexual control groups and no child assessments.[54]

Inadequate control

Where control groups were used, studies usually compared children in divorced lesbian mother-headed families with children in divorced heterosexual mother-headed families. This is understandable, in that both groups have undergone experience of parental separation or divorce, and lack a father. Comparisons with unbroken heterosexual two-parent families are rare and more conspicuous by their absence. Robert Lerner and Althea Nagai found only four studies in 49 comparing lesbian parents to the traditional heterosexual household, and two of these failed to distinguish lesbians living with and without 'partners'.[55] This makes it difficult to say how 'gay' or lesbian upbringing compares with that by married couples, and rules out any possible generalisations to the wider population. At best, these studies show that children in lesbian households do no worse than those in father-absent, heterosexual lone-parent households – if we accept the deductions and conclusion of the researchers. Subjects from both types of family may be atypical in comparison with their counterparts raised in heterosexual homes with both mother and father present.

Very small samples

Studies of homosexual parenting often have very small sample populations. This may mean that effects of homosexual rearing are not picked up. Since these cannot reach statistical significance with very limited numbers of subjects, the results are entirely inconclusive. Attempts to introduce even the most basic of controls, e.g. for gender of children, subdivide some samples even further. (It would be impossible to tell if a particular disease, which might strike one in 40 people overall, occurred more in some groups than others if sample sizes were so small, say 20 in each, that people with the disease are unlikely to be picked up in the first place.) All but one of Robert Lerner's and Althea Nagai's 49 studies "suffer from having samples...so small that the statistical tests used have extremely low power...there is a high probability that the results are deemed non-significant...simply due to the fact that the samples they use are too small."[56]

Hypothetical children

Little research goes beyond childhood, and few would expect significant differences between children to be as apparent in early life as they might be in adolescence or adulthood. Some studies used as the basis of claims that children raised by homosexuals do not differ, or are superior to, those raised by heterosexuals, do not even involve actual children, but reactions of mothers to hypothetical situations involving children.[57] Although assertions about the worth of homosexual parenting typically refer to 'gay fathers' alongside lesbian mothers, there have been no available studies to date comparing children raised in male homosexual households, or by expressly 'gay' fathers, with children raised by heterosexuals.

Recently Helen Barrett and Fiona Tasker asserted that their "findings lend little support to predications from traditional theories of child development concerning the effects of gay parents on their children".[58] However, their investigations of 'gay fathers' comprises a postal survey of 101 men recruited through adverts in the gay press and from local and national gay groups. The sample was therefore entirely unrepresentative and involved no study of children; only "...gay and bisexual men's perceptions of their children's responses to having a gay parent...". The children were not asked by post or otherwise.

While Gillian A. Dunne's study was celebrated in the press with the headlines 'Gay Men Make Better Fathers', her 'gay' dads sample included 14 per cent 'donor dads' and eight per cent 'social dads' (whose biological relationship to the child or children is obscure). Eleven per cent were 'wannabee dads' and therefore not fathers at all.[59] Again all are volunteer respondents and thus not representative of any population. There is no investigation of children so we have no clue how they are actually faring. Dunne interviews some of the currently married 'gay' dads, who give glowing self-justifying accounts of their parenting skills. If this says anything about anything, then it is about people staying together in reasonable harmony for the sake of the children and thus, for the value of marriage for child rearing.

In turn, there is <u>no</u> available research on adopted children brought up by lesbian or gay parents. As positive 'evidence', all the Children's Society can offer are three cases in the public domain which went to the High Court, and a favourable letter from a solicitor, who has acted in 10 adoption and fostering placements involving gay and lesbian people.[60]

Volunteer samples with vested interests

In most studies the subjects are self selected volunteers (often recruited through homosexual publications). There are no studies of child development based on random, representative samples. Educated, economically secure white lesbians who "reside in relatively progressive urban centers, most often in California or the Northeastern states," are over-represented in the research.[61] Laura Lott-Whitehead and Carol T. Tully's study is not untypical[62] in that the respondents were "well educated white women with high incomes who lived in Georgia"; obtained by "contacting various gay and lesbian organisations and the researcher's personal and professional friends..." and had a response rate of 24.6 per cent. In turn, studies recruiting control groups draw heavily from sources that are extremely unrepresentative of single heterosexual mothers, or from pressure group newsletters and feminist publications. As Lerner and Nagai have said: "There is no way one can make population estimates on volunteer samples of anything. It has nothing to do with discrimination or stigmatization of homosexuals. It has everything to do with the basic distinction between a probability and non-probability sample." A bigger sample of volunteers will not give a better population picture than a small sample.[63] No matter how large the number of respondents, findings from non-random surveys cannot be generalised and they have no valid implications for matters of public policy.

For various reasons, random samples may not be possible, or very expensive and time consuming to set up, not least because of the rarity of same-sex parenting in the population. However, if this makes pair matching necessary, it may result in a further loss of cases where comparable individuals from the heterosexual population cannot be found. Sometimes the ways in which groups or individuals are matched is unclear or very inexact in same-sex parenting reports, even when it comes to matters like the ages of children or mothers.

Not least, with non-random samples of volunteers, there is bias, fuelled by "...lesbians' political and legal desire to present a happy, well-adjusted family to the world."[64] The aim is advocacy and affirmation in the name of scientific research. The volunteers to such 'samples of convenience' know the purpose of the research and have an interest in the outcome. So have the researchers, who are overwhelmingly sympathetic to the homosexual movement. Researchers who may have reservations about homosexual parenting, or are simply not positively committed or predisposed to this, may be felt not to have the appropriate rapport with homosexuals. This leaves the field open to activists – who control the source and presentation of reports, so that the public and those in a position to influence policy tend to get research results from highly partisan sources. As observed by Belcastro and colleagues:

> "...based upon the researchers' interpretation of the data and at least in one case censorship of the data, most [studies] were biased towards proving homosexual parents were fit parents. A disturbing revelation was that some of the published works had to disregard their own results in order to conclude that homosexuals were fit parents. We believe that the system of manuscript review by peers, for minimum scientific standards of research, was compromised in several of these studies."[65]

An aside: 'file-drawer' studies

We do not know, in this as in other sensitive areas, about the extent of unpublished work, or the existence of 'file-drawer' studies. Researchers are acutely aware that, even while they may be scrupulously scientific over reaching and presenting their findings, some outcomes are more politically acceptable than others. Again, this is not just a problem in this area of family research. However, it has come about that, for same-sex parenting research to be acceptable, this must come from a pro-gay standpoint, and that anything coming from a pro-gay researcher is often now taken to be of unquestionable scientific status. This puts the results beyond criticism. The only reason anyone might disagree, find fault with any research, or examine its assertions, comes about because they are bigoted, or homophobic and heterosexist.

Failure to allow for other causes

In the best of circumstances, it is unlikely that a study group and its comparison group are going to be identical except for the independent variable under investigation. Thus the need for controls on extraneous and suppressor variables: those most familiar will be occupation, income, education, age, race and so forth. Such controls increase the possibility that any changes in the dependent variable are due to differences in the independent variable, rather than other, or third, variables which are masking the true relationship. Robert Lerner and Althea Nagai found that the "bulk of the studies either failed to control for these most basic demographic variables or controlled for them improperly."[66] "Even the most statistically sophisticated homosexual parenting study we examined overlooks the importance of suppressor effects…".[67] That 'most statistically sophisticated' study was the Sperm Bank of California study.[68] The authors found no significant differences in analyses of the relationship between parental sexual orientation and the child's behaviour, when controlling for relationships within the family and the parent's mental health. However, here as elsewhere, homosexual parents had significantly more education, and it is known that parental education is positively related to child outcomes. So

> "if lesbian and heterosexual mothers produce similar child outcomes to their heterosexual counterparts even where the lesbians are better educated, it may well be the case that when educational levels are properly equated that heterosexual mothers produce more favourable outcomes...however, education is not entered into subsequent equations, and therefore remains an un-addressed potential suppressor."[69]

Despite finding significant differences for extraneous variables, a whole number of important studies fail to take the next step, which is to enter or allow for these in subsequent statistical analysis. This cannot but make any subsequent analyses and conclusions invalid. Only one of Lerner and Nagai's studies "even came close to addressing this issue, and that study failed to even report which variables were dropped or added in its analysis."[70]

One of the foremost researchers on same-sex parenting has herself recently summarised the poor state of research. So far "no study has contained a large sample of children and few studies have controlled sample characteristics sufficiently to permit confident generalisations".[71]

Epilogue: campaigners counter-attack

Attack being a way of defence, campaigners for homosexual parenting like to accuse their perceived opponents of being the ones really doing the biased or bad research:

> "What kinds of home environments best foster children's psychological adjustment and growth? No question is more central to the field of child development research. Historically, researchers in the United States have

often supposed that the most favourable home environments are provided by white, middle-class, two-parent families, in which the father is paid to work outside the home but the mother is not. Although rarely stated explicitly, it has most often been assumed that both parents in such families are heterosexual."[72]

In reality, "researchers in the United States" have not just "supposed that the most favourable home environments" are provided by this parody. They have shown, by evidence from correctly conducted studies, that the two-parent, conjugal family tends to come out ahead of 'alternatives' in terms of outcomes for children.[73] This has not been made up. Moreover, they have assumed that two-parent families contain adults of opposite sexes, since that is what they are, in the same way that there are other givens of the natural world where, for example, pigs do not fly. Are we to believe, for example, that the married couples in the main longitudinal studies like the National Child Development Study in the UK or the Longitudinal Survey of Youth in the US, are predominantly people in drag who have secretly mastered some method of self-fertilisation or pathogenesis, or are using marriage on a wholesale basis as a cover for homosexual activity with third parties?

A related account blames the deficiencies of same-sex parenting research on "the social fact of heterosexism" or that children, biologically and often socially, have two parents of different sexes. This arbitrary cultural imposition which, together with the resultant "pervasiveness of social prejudice and institutionalised discrimination against lesbians and gay men" has "operated to constrain the research populations, concepts and designs…".[74] Apparently, "the field suffers…from the unfortunate intellectual consequences that follow from the implicit hetero-normative presumption…that healthy child development depends on parenting by a married heterosexual couple". While it is admitted that "few contributors to this literature personally subscribe to this view", they are so cowed by anti-gay sentiment that they ask "whether lesbigay [sic] parents subject their children to greater risks or harm than are confronted by children reared by heterosexual parents." The bias in the research for finding that everything is fine with same-sex parenting is the fault of "anti-gay scholars seek[ing] evidence of harm", who make "sympathetic researchers defensively stress its absence."[75] Thus, on the one hand only anti-gay prejudice makes anyone ask how same-sex parents compare with others in the first place, instead of assuming that all outcomes are fine in any circumstances, while on the other hand, prejudice makes researchers pretend that outcomes are all equal! The way forward is to move beyond 'hetero-normality', since "homophobia and discrimination are the chief reasons why parental sexual orientation matters at all."[76] Otherwise, anything is and should be acceptable. Differences in outcomes for children "cannot be considered deficits from any legitimate public policy perspective. They either favor the children with lesbigay parents, are secondary effects of social prejudice, or represent 'just a difference' of the sort democratic societies should respect and protect."[77]

Endnotes:

[1] This has been noted even by authors who take a pro-homosexual stance, for example Bigner, J J and Bozett, F W, 'Parenting by Gay Fathers', *Marriage and Family Review*, 14, 1990, page 165

[2] Cameron, P and Cameron, K, 'Homosexual Parents', *Op cit*, page 768; and Tyas, S L and Pederson, L L, 'Psychosocial Factors Related to Adolescent Smoking: a Critical Review of the Literature', *Tobacco Control*, 7(4), 1998, pages 409-420

[3] The Children's Society, *Information on the Children's Society Change of Policy on Adoption and Fostering*, August 1999, page 6

[4] Triseliotis J, Shireman, J and Hundleby, M, *Adoption: Theory, Policy and Practice*, Cassell, London, 1997, page 219

[5] American Psychological Association et al, brief in case of Bottoms v Bottoms, 27 December 1994, page 19

[6] *Ibid*, page 25

[7] Patterson, C J, 'Children of Lesbian and Gay Parents', *Op cit*, page 1036

[8] *Ibid*, page 1038

[9] Lott-Whitehead, L and Tully, C T, 'The Family Lives of Lesbian Mothers', *Op cit*, page 254

[10] Cameron, P and Cameron, K, 'Homosexual Parents', *Op cit*, page 759

[11] Cameron, P, 'Homosexual Parents: Testing "Common Sense" – a Literature Review emphasizing the Golombok and Tasker Longitudinal Study of Lesbians' Children', *Psychological Reports*, 85, 1999, page 283

[12] Cameron, P, 'Homosexual Parents: Their Children Testify', Unpublished paper, *Family Research Institute,* 1999, page 2

[13] See for example: Joshi, H et al, *Children 5-16* Research Briefing No 6, January 2000, Economic and Social Research Council, University of Hull

[14] Buchanan, A and Brinke, J T, *Op cit*, pages 52-53

[15] Lempers J D, Clark-Lempers, D and Simons, R L, 'Economic Hardship, Parenting and Distress in Adolescence', *Child Development*, 60, 1989, pages 25-39;
Takeuchi D T, Williams, D R and Adair, R K, 'Economic Stress in the Family and Children's Emotional and Behavioural Problems', *Journal of Marriage and the Family*, 53, 1991, pages 1031-41; and
Jones, L, 'Unemployment and Child Abuse', *Families in Society: The Journal of Contemporary Human Services*, 1990, pages 579-88.

[16] Dawson, D A, 'Family Structure and Children's Health, United States 1988',

Vital and Health Statistics, Series 10, US Department of Health and Human Services, 1991, pages 3-6 and 26-41

17   The Children's Society, *Op cit*, page 6

18   Gartner, R, 'Family Structure, Welfare Spending, and Child Homicide in Developed Democracies', *Journal of Marriage and The Family*, 53, 1991, pages 231-240;
and see for example, Morgan P, *'Farewell to the Family? Public Policy and Family Breakdown in Britain and the USA'*, The IEA Health and Welfare Unit, 1999 (Second Edition), chapter 5

19   Daly, M, and Wilson, M, 'Evolution and Human Sciences', *The Times Higher Educational Supplement*, 25 June 1993;
Daly, M, and Wilson, M, *The Truth About Cinderella, A Darwinian view of parental love*, Weidenfeld and Nicolson, London, 1998, pages 26-36

20   Gordon, M, and Creighton, S J, 'Natal and Non-natal Fathers as Sexual Abusers in the United Kingdom: a Comparative Analysis', *Journal of Marriage and the Family*, 50, 1988, pages 99-105

21   (84 per cent of all cases of non-parental child abuse in a prominent study happened to children from lone-parent homes.)
Margolin, L, 'Child Abuse by Mothers' Boyfriends: Why the Overrepresentation?', *Child Abuse and Neglect*, 16, 1992, pages 541-551

22   *Sex and America's Teenagers,* Alan Guttmacher Institute, New York and Washington, 1994, pages 22, 23, 28

23   Freund K, Heasman G, Racansky, I G and Glancy, G, 'Pedophilia and hetero-sexuality vs. homosexuality', *Journal of Sex and Marital Therapy*, 10(3), 1984, pages 193-200
Grubin, D, *Sex offending against children: understanding the risk,* Home Office, Police Research Series, Paper 99, 1998, page 14

24   Triseliotis J, Shireman, J and Hundleby, M, *Op cit*, page 220

25   Weatherburn, P et al, *The Sexual Lifestyles of Gay and Bisexual Men in England and Wales,* HMSO, 1992, page 13
All the men in this study were under 21. So given this last statistic the partner involved was either more than 10 years *younger* (that is the partner is a child under the age of 11), or more likely a man more than 10 years *older.* Such a case could involve a 10 year old boy being seduced by a 25 year old man.

26   Hickson, F C I et al, 'Gay Men as Victims of Nonconsensual Sex', *Archives of Sexual Behaviour,* 23(3), 1994, page 28

27   *Criminal Statistics England and Wales 1999,* HMSO, Table 2.16, page 50

and Wellings, K et al, *Sexual Behaviour in Britain- The National Survey of Sexual Attitudes and Lifestyles,* Penguin Books, 1994, page 209.
In the UK, 86.5 per cent of men have had intercourse only with a woman in the past year, 0.7 per cent have had intercourse only with a man and 0.4 per cent with both a man and a woman. Even if the bisexuals are counted as homosexuals, resulting in a figure of 1.1 per cent, heterosexuals outnumber homosexuals by 78 to 1. If bisexuals were not included at all or counted with the heterosexuals the ratio would be over 120 to 1 in both cases.
Having considered the 'pool' of heterosexuals and homosexual it is now possible to evaluate the rape figures. In 1999/00 there were 8,409 rapes – 7,809 of women (92.9 per cent of the total) – and 600 of men (7.1 per cent). The ratio of homosexual rapes to heterosexual rapes is therefore 7,809/600 = 13.0 to 1. But there is one homosexual person for every 78 heterosexual persons. Homosexual rapes are therefore six times over-represented in the reported rape figures. (The real figure must be higher since the calculation has counted all bisexuals as homosexuals).
The new National Survey of Sexual Attitudes and Lifestyles was published at the time of going to press. Its sample size is smaller, 11,000, and it excludes the age range 45-59, used in the 1990 survey. A similar calculation shows homosexual rapes to be nearly three times over-represented in the overall rape figures. Johnson, A M et al, 'Sexual Behaviour in Britain: Partnerships, Practices and HIV Risk Behaviours', *The Lancet*, 358, December 2001, pages 1835-1841.

[28] Waterhouse Report *Lost in Care,* Report of the Tribunal of Inquiry into the abuse of children in care in the former county council areas of Gwynedd and Clwyd since 1974, The Stationery Office, 15 February 2000, Chapter 52, part 52.71-52.73

[29] See, for example, accounts of child abuse resulting from employment policies of Islington Council in the 1980s: *Guardian,* 3 March 2001 and 16 February 2000; also *Financial Times*, 17 December 1999

[30] Logan, B, 'A submission, with special reference to de facto & same-sex couples, on the Law Commission's "Adoption: options for Reform"', *New Zealand Education Development Foundation*, Preliminary Paper 38, 18 January 2000

[31] Lerner, R and Nagai, A K, 'No Basis: What the Studies Don't Tell Us About Same-Sex Parenting', Marriage Law Project, Washington D C, 2001, pages 7-8

[32] Cameron, P, 'Homosexual Parents: Testing "Common Sense" – a Literature

Review emphasizing the Golombok and Tasker Longitudinal Study of Lesbians' Children', *Op cit*, page 284

33 Lerner, R and Nagai, A K, *Op cit*, page 6

34 *Ibid*, page 7

35 Logan, B, *Op cit*

36 'Lesbians who set up home with 'pickle jar babies' have split', *The Daily Telegraph*, 31 July 1998

37 Family Policy Studies Centre, *Families and Adoption*, Family Briefing Paper 14, September 2000 citing Hicks, J and McDermott, J, *Op cit*, for *Adoption Now: A Solution for Looked after Children?* An International Seminar, London, 5 July 2001

38 See conclusions in Amato, P R and Booth, A, *A Generation at Risk,* Harvard University Press, 1997, pages 219-221

39 *Record (Northern New Jersey)*, 7 July 1992

40 *San Francisco Chronicle*, 20 October 1988

41 *Miami Herald*, 12 January 1990

42 Lerner, R and Nagai, A K, *Op cit*, pages 11, 13

43 *Ibid*, page 16

44 *Loc cit*

45 *Ibid*, page 19

46 *Ibid*, pages 20-21

47 *Ibid*, page 27

48 Belcastro, P A et al, 'A Review of Data Based Studies Addressing the Affects of Homosexual Parenting on Children's Sexual and Social Functioning', *Journal of Divorce and Remarriage*, 20(1/2), 1993, pages 105-121

49 *Ibid*, page 119

50 Gold M A, Perrin E C, Futterman, D and Friedman, S B, 'Children of Gay or Lesbian Parents', *Pediatrics in Review*, 15(9), 1994, page 357

51 Golombok, S and Tasker, F 'Children in Lesbian and Gay Families: Theories and Evidence', *Annual Review of Sex Research* 5, 1994, page 94 referring to Patterson, C J, 'Children of Lesbian and Gay Parents', *Op cit*, pages 1025-1042

52 Belcastro, P A et al, *Op cit*, page 116

53 Lerner, R and Nagai, A K, *Op cit*, page 27

54 *Ibid*, pages 87-89 in reference to Koepke, L et al, 'Relationship Quality in a Sample of Lesbian Couples with Children and Child-free Lesbian Couples', *Family Relations*, 41, 1992, pages 224-229

55 Lerner, R and Nagai, A K, *Op cit*, page 49

[56] *Ibid*, page 99

[57] See for example: Flaks D K, Ficher I, Masterpasqua, F and Joseph, G, 'Lesbians Choosing Motherhood: A Comparative Study of Lesbian and Heterosexual Parents and their Children', *Developmental Psychology* 31(1), 1995, pages 105-114; and:
Miller J A, Jacobsen, R B and Bigner, J J, 'The Child's Home Environment for Lesbian vs Heterosexual Mothers: A Neglected Area of Research', *Journal of Homosexuality* 7(1), 1981, pages 49-56

[58] Barrett, H and Tasker, F, 'Growing up with a Gay Parent: Views of 101 Gay Fathers on their Sons' and Daughters' Experiences', *Educational and Child Psychology*, 18(1), 2001, page 75

[59] Dunne, G, *The Different Dimensions of Gay Fatherhood: Exploding the Myths*, London School of Economics Discussion Paper Series, January 2000, page 4 and *Scotland on Sunday*, 9 January 2000

[60] The Children's Society, *Op cit*, page 5

[61] Stacey, J and Biblarz, T J, *Op cit*, page 166

[62] Lott-Whitehead, L and Tully, C T, 'The Family Lives of Lesbian Mothers', *Op cit*, pages 246-247

[63] Lerner, R and Nagai, A K, *Op cit*, page 71

[64] Belcastro, P A et al, *Op cit*, page 116

[65] *Ibid*, page 117

[66] Lerner, R and Nagai, A K, *Op cit*, page 44

[67] *Ibid*, page 34

[68] Chan R W, Raboy, B and Patterson, C J, 'Psychological Adjustment among Children Conceived via Donor Insemination by Lesbian and Heterosexual Mothers', *Child Development*, 69(2), 1998, pages 443-457

[69] Lerner, R and Nagai, A K, *Op cit*, page 34 referring to Chan R W, Raboy, B and Patterson, C J, *Op cit*, pages 443-457

[70] Lerner, R and Nagai, A K, *Op cit*, page 52

[71] Barrett, H and Tasker, F, *Op cit*, page 74

[72] Patterson, C J, 'Children of Lesbian and Gay Parents', *Op cit*, page 1025

[73] See for example: Amato, P R and Booth, A, *A Generation at Risk*, *Op cit*, pages 219-220; and Dawson, D A, *Op cit*, pages 3-6 and 26-41

[74] Stacey, J and Biblarz, T J, *Op cit*, pages 160-161

[75] *Ibid*, page 160

[76] *Ibid*, page 177

[77] *Loc cit*

Chapter 3

The prominent studies

Studies of same-sex parenting not only suffer from defective design, technique and analyses. Despite repeated assertions to the contrary, many studies actually indicate significant differences between homosexual and heterosexual parenting outcomes for children, <u>particularly</u> the likelihood that children of homosexuals may become involved in homosexual behaviour themselves. This emerges from any scrutiny of the most prominent and oft quoted studies such as those of the lesbian families undertaken by Susan Golombok and colleagues.

Golombok, S, Children in Lesbian and Single-parent Households, 1983

Two groups, of 27 each of lesbian and heterosexual lone-parent mothers (without cohabitees), were recruited through gay and lone-parent publications. (The self-selected sample immediately calls into question any generalisability of the findings.) It seems that a bisexual woman might be assigned to either the experimental or the control group (at least five of the 27 women in the lesbian group were bisexual). The experimental lesbian group contained women living in a variety of parenting households – nine lived alone with their child(ren), 12 with another woman, others were in "mixed shared households", lesbian shared households, or part of a lesbian couple sharing the home with the husband.[1] Lesbian families had nearly twice as many female children as male children, while the opposite pertained with the control group. Nearly a half of the lesbian women had received psychiatric care, along with 18.5 per cent of the women in the control group. Most of the parents in both groups had been married and the children were mainly nine to 10 years old at the time of interview. They had averaged five years of age at the break-up of their parents' marriages. While more of the lesbian women had further education or training or were in professional occupations, there appears to be no or minimal controls made for socio-economic status, or class and income. There had been marked marital discord or hostility during the year preceding marital break-up for about two-thirds of cases in each group.

Adaptations of standardized interviews were utilised with no revised assessment of validity or assessment of inter-rater reliability.[2] In both groups the scores were broadly similar for gender identity, sex-typed behaviour, and sexual object choice.[3] Children's emotions, behaviour and relationships were assessed on parents and teachers questionnaires used for epidemiological studies. Scores of 13 or more on the particular parental scale or of nine or more on the teachers scale are usually indicative of significant difficulties. In this study the proportions of children scoring at or above these cut off points was 33.3 per cent of boys and 16.6 per cent of girls in the lesbian group on the teacher's scale and 15.3 per cent of boys and 12.5 per cent of girls on the parental scale. The comparative figures for the heterosexual lone-parent group were 36.3 per cent and 28.5 per cent respectively on the teacher's scale and 25 per cent and 35.7 per cent respectively on the parental scale. The teacher's questionnaire was not applied to more than a quarter of the children in the lesbian group. There were no reported differences of any significance in the ability to make peer relationships.

While there seemed to be somewhat greater psychiatric disorder in the heterosexual lone-parent group, both groups score very high for problems. A baseline figure gives seven per cent of children generally from the Isle of Wight using the same scales, and 25 per cent of boys, and 13 per cent of girls, living in Inner London. Children in the public care tend to score highest.[4] Foster children in placement for on average about five years, mostly starting before the age of five, scored 30 per cent; with the figures moving down to 11 per cent for children adopted by their foster parents.[5] A similar study for children in long-term foster care showed ratings for disturbance of nearly 40 per cent.[6] There is a general consensus that roughly 10-15 per cent of younger children have mild to moderate disorders according to checklists commonly used to define internalising and externalising problems.[7] In one prominent study in London, 15 per cent of the sample met cut-off criteria for mild problems and seven per cent were seen as having moderate to severe problems.[8] In a survey carried out in 1999 for the Department of Health, 10 per cent of children aged five to 15 years had a mental disorder. (Among five to 10 year olds, 10 per cent of boys and six per cent of girls had a mental disorder. In 11-15 year olds, the proportions of children with any mental disorder were 13 per cent for boys and 10 per cent for girls.)[9]

Kirkpatrick, M, Lesbian Mothers and their Children, 1981

Another much quoted study has been that of M. Kirkpatrick and colleagues,[10] using interviews with mothers to detect common childhood disorders, and the same basic teachers' scales for children's emotional and behavioural problems used by Golombok and colleagues. It is widely reported that, in relation to population norms, the children of lesbian mothers were no more likely to show emotional or behavioural problems than were children in heterosexual families. However, the study seemed to attract an inordinate proportion of disturbed children due to the investigators offering mothers a complete evaluation and feedback of their child's psychological profile in exchange for their participation in the study. The result was that the study sample consisted of 60 per cent moderately and severely disturbed subjects. Such a proportion of disturbed children is hardly representative of any population of children, wherever or however raised.

Tasker, F and Golombok, S, Adults Raised as Children in Lesbian Families, 1995

Most studies of homosexual childrearing, with the exception of those focussing on sexual orientation, have concerned younger children, rather than adolescents or adults. Fiona Tasker and Susan Golombok returned to their original sample[11] when the children were adults aged 17-35 years. Only 46 could be interviewed out of the original 78, a response rate of 62 per cent of the earlier study. Those left in the follow-up were weighted even more in favour of lesbian mothers with further education (13 out of 18), compared to lone heterosexual mothers (five out of 16). Young adults from lesbian families were said to be no more likely than those from heterosexual lone-parent homes to have sought professional help for mental health problems. However, non-participants in the follow-up were more likely than participants to have experienced a period of separation from their mother, which included periods in care. Within the lesbian group, children whose mothers reported greater interpersonal conflict with their cohabitee were also less likely to participate. Moreover, after 14 years of different living arrangements, the two groups of children had exchanged places, with the lesbians' children scoring less mentally fit on three measures of mental health, even though the attrition of the sample favoured the lesbians. The authors' attitude to such change has also been noted: "It is interesting that, when the differences were in favor of the lesbians' children, Tasker and Golombok used them to underscore the direction; ...when the differences were not in favor of the lesbians' children...these 'fell within the normal range' or 'were no more likely than'."[12] Given that the statistical tests used assume random samples and independence of subjects, the findings of 'no difference' might simply have meant that the sample was too small, biased or the assessments faulty. "In such cases, finding no statistically significant differences between small samples of clustered volunteers – unlike not finding differences between two large random samples – is, from a scientific standpoint, probably uninterpretable".[13] As we saw, there were very high rates of problems in both groups earlier in life. Well-conducted studies are remarkably consistent in indicating that children identified as having mental health problems early in life have a high probability of continuing to show difficulties up into adolescence: usually around 50:50.[14] Yet, in this study, the correlation between the 'mental health' scores of the children at age 10 as rated by teachers and parents and their having visited a mental health professional 14 years later was zero.[15]

At follow up, all but one of the original group of lone heterosexual mothers were reported by their children to have had at least one relationship, usually cohabitational.[16] The same was so for lesbians, although young adults in lesbian households purportedly described their 'step-relationships' more positively than did those raised by a heterosexual mother and her new partner. There is speculation that children from lesbian households could more easily accept a step-parent in their home because she need not be seen as a direct competitor to the absent father. However, it is important to remember that the comparison between follow-up participants and non participants indicated that the sample may have lost the children from lesbian backgrounds whose mothers reported less positive relationships with their female partner.[17]

Their findings are said to give little support to the view that children's peer relationships would be adversely affected by being raised in a lesbian family. The lesbian children were reported not to have incurred peer stigmatisation at adolescence, or to have been more teased and bullied by peers, than those from heterosexual single-parent homes – although they were more likely to report peer teasing about their own sexuality. However, the actual figures are that 48 per cent of the lesbians' children reported prolonged teasing, compared to 33 per cent of the lone-mothers' children. Also, 36 per cent of the lesbians' children had been specifically teased about their mothers' lifestyle, and 44 per cent recalled having been teased about being lesbian or gay themselves, compared to 14 and 19 per cent respectively in the heterosexual group. Of the 24 adult children for whom results were available, one was still unaware of her mother's lesbianism, five "successfully concealed their mother's sexual orientation," 14 "felt comfortable enough to tell at least one close friend, either directly or by not hiding the situation", and four "had met with a negative reaction from friends (although in two cases the friends later became more positive)".[18] There is no parallel among the children of heterosexual lone-mothers. In line with their upbeat account, Tasker and Golombok also reported that the children from the lesbian group were 'generally positive' about their family identity, although it is admitted that retrospective reports indicated less positive feelings about their lesbian family identity during adolescence. This is attributed to "...the context of widespread prejudice against lesbian women and gay men."[19] The authors claim that:

> "Young adults brought up in lesbian families were more likely to be proud of their mother's sexual identity. They often viewed this as a political matter and would seek to inform public opinion on gay rights by giving their own family history. In contrast, young people from non-married heterosexual backgrounds tended to regard their mother's lifestyle as her personal choice and its details as a private family matter. Although the majority accepted their mother's identity as a single parent or as a remarried mother and were happy to talk about it with friends, none thought of it as an issue that they would be proud to discuss with casual acquaintances."[20]

To which one might reply, 'Why should they?' And, if they did, would it not be 'heterosexist'? Homosexuals define themselves in terms of their sexual identity, and the children of homosexuals are more likely to be actively encouraged by the parent to adopt the gay outlook. Moreover, is there a good reason why anybody has to endorse anywhere they end up as a positive choice or lifestyle? As this may be far from what they wanted or expected, it may be honesty, rather than inadequacy, that is reflected when children "brought up by non-married heterosexual mothers were more likely to report that their mother was negative about her nontraditional identity and preferred to be married."[21]

Problems with peers?

Susan Golombok and colleagues' material – or rather, their interpretation of the material – is incongruent with many other same-sex parenting studies. These indicate that children, principally adolescents, experience relationship problems with other people because of their actual or potential knowledge of their parents' homosexuality.

In summaries of existing work by pro-gay commentators, the relationship of the child to the outside world is expressly identified as a recurrent problem:

> "...[children] commonly fear that other children will find out that their mother is a lesbian... Out of fear of discovery of their mothers' homosexuality, these children can become anxious, withdrawn, hypervigilant, or secretive, and may attempt to control their mothers' behaviour. Some children, particularly as they approach their teens, shy away from friends and refuse to bring them home out of concern that someone will 'find out'."[22]

"This awareness frequently occurs after seven years of age and intensifies during pubescence and the early teenage years"[23] – even if it does not take the extreme form of the girl in the lesbian step-family who became electively mute so that she would not have to share the family's 'secret' with others.[24] Commenting on a comparison of 26 children of lesbians with 28 of divorced heterosexual mothers, G.A. Javaid observed that most of the children had reservations about having a homosexual mother and how:

"The majority of the children said that they would not tell their peers about their mother's lesbianism. Some said they had traded their secret with a best friend, who they knew would not betray them. Apart from maintaining a general attitude of secrecy, children volunteered more specific concerns, including the following: the fear of mother losing custody; choosing to live with Dad because 'I couldn't cope with it'; 'lost a friend because Mom is gay'; peers' name-calling and teasing; a desire to hide all signs of Mum's homosexuality; a wish that she wasn't a lesbian or her lover wasn't there; using euphemisms, e.g., calling her lover a room-mate."[25]

Shame and embarrassment may result in a retreat into secrecy, where the children assume the responsibility of hiding the truth about their parents' sexual preferences from friends, classmates and others.[26] In Ann O'Connell's study of 11 adolescents with lesbian mothers, the "theme of losing friends or being judged was expressed by each young person with a moderate to high level of intensity". They may be "keeping their mother's lesbianism a secret to shield their friends from embarrassment and discomfort" and, for boys, "...to defend themselves against being thought of as different."[27] Self-imposed isolation tends to exaggerate the feeling of difference these children may already experience.[28] One investigator reported that nearly 60 per cent of the children of lesbian mothers and over 20 per cent of the children of 32 gay fathers experienced relationships problems with other people because of the knowledge of their parents' homosexuality. This centred on how to present the parental sexual orientation to others and fears about peer ostracism (although far less actually experienced any discrimination according to parental reports).[29] In another study of 21 children of eight lesbians, the researcher reported how several boys were "...furious, not, they claimed, at their mother's homosexuality, but at her lover." Others "were embarrassed by the stereotypical 'butch-femme' relationship they thought the two women had. This seemed to be a thin veil over their bruised self-esteem."[30] In turn, few of the children in 34 lesbian families studied by L. Rafkin, reported no psychological or social difficulties.[31]

Since almost every child:

> "...talks about keeping mom's lesbianism a secret, from school friends, from neighbours, and sometimes from other family members... It was difficult to discover just how many children carry the burden of social stigma... All but a few of the children...keep their mother's sexual preference from someone, for all or part of their lives, even if they live in places like San Francisco... Many kids said it was difficult to bring friends home because of lesbian books and other 'paraphernalia'...the lack of stable long-term relationships is difficult for any kid."[32]

In Sotirios Sarantakos' comparative Australian study of the children of married couples, heterosexual and homosexual cohabitees,[33] many living with homosexual couples were said to avoid involvement in group activities or out-of-school activities generally, or any kind of talking about home life. They were also reported to feel uncomfortable with others of a sex different from the people they lived with, to be distant, careful and overly polite, and to be considered by teachers to be 'loners' or 'introverts'. "Experiences in their personal and family life were thought to have motivated them to avoid working with and relying on others, and to mistrust other children in the case of children of lesbians, [this meant] males in particular."[34] They tended to be ridiculed and harassed by other children. Not only were they described as " 'more confused about their gender' than children of heterosexual couples", but they also found "...it difficult to be fully accepted by their peers as boys or girls." Children going through such experiences "...suffered significantly in social and emotional terms, but also in terms of scholastic achievement and have developed negative attitudes to school and learning. These children found it very difficult to adjust in school, to trust friends inside and outside the school, and to join peer groups in general."[35] Pro-gay researchers put all of this down to the "profound impact of a homophobic culture".[36] However, children have their own preferences and children are very conservative. As mentioned by Ivan Massow, prominent gay businessman:

"Many parents I talked to expressed concerns as their child went through a phase of noticing, usually in the company of their schoolfriends, that they were missing something that everyone else had... One very good friend of mine, probably the best mother I know, found this problem very difficult to deal with because kids aren't PC. They just want to know which one is their dad."[37]

More likely to be gay?

While Susan Golombok and colleagues claim that no significant differences were found between young adults from lesbian and heterosexual mother households in the proportions who had experienced sexual attraction to someone of the same gender, the actual figures are nine out of 25 and four out of 21 respectively. Young adults raised by lesbians were significantly more likely to have had a sexual relationship with someone of the same gender. No children of heterosexual mothers had experienced a gay or lesbian relationship, but six children of lesbians (one male and 5 females), became involved in one or more sexual relationships with a partner of the same gender and two women from lesbian backgrounds were currently in lesbian relationships and identified themselves as lesbian. Four out of seven sons, and 10 of 15 daughters of lesbians were significantly more likely to report having considered the possibility of a lesbian or gay relationship, compared to only two of 10 sons and one of eight daughters of heterosexual controls. The researchers observe that:

"It cannot be ruled out that the outcomes for these young people would have been the same had they been raised by parents who were genetically unrelated to them (e.g. adoptive parents). However, the results suggest that the group difference in same-gender sexual interest is a consequence of the children's experiences with lesbian and heterosexual mothers while growing up, particularly in view of the finding that the childhood family environments of young adults from lesbian families who reported same-gender sexual interest were characterised by an openness and acceptance of a lesbian lifestyle."[38]

When asked what they thought their mothers' desires were regarding their sexual preferences, 56 per cent of lesbians' daughters said they believed their mother wanted them to be homosexual (compared to none of the heterosexuals' daughters), and 25 per cent said that they believed that their mother wanted them to be heterosexual.[39] The more accepting the mother was of homosexuality in her children, the more frequent her children's homosexual interest.[40] The children may not necessarily want to be gay. In Ann O'Connell's study, nine of the 11 young people "remembered worrying about becoming gay and most often cited reasons such as fear of being judged and the intensely felt wish to be 'normal'… Fears of becoming homosexual abated for all these young people once dating began. One young woman reminisced about early dating: 'There was a hint of relief. I thought, good, I like guys!'"[41]

Bearing the limitations of the studies in mind, if there are any differences between children raised by lesbian mothers versus heterosexual mothers, then it is in gender identity and sexual behaviour. Stonewall asserts that, insofar as there are concerns that children will be confused about their sexual and gender identity, or teased and picked on at school: "There is no evidence that this is the case and a growing body of research shows that children in lesbian and gay families are no different from children growing up in heterosexual households".[42] This is simply wrong. Indeed, pro-gay commentators Judith Stacey and Timothy Biblarz observe how "[v]irtually all of the published research claims to find no differences in the sexuality of children reared by lesbigay [sic] parents and those reared by nongay parents – but none of the studies…attempts to theorize about such an implausible outcome" – a 'reticence' ascribed to the oppressive impact of heterosexism on gay research.[43] As it is, from their own scrutiny of the findings from 21 studies they considered best equipped to address questions about how parental sexual orientation matters to children's development, they conclude that "on some dimensions…related to gender and sexuality – the sexual orientations of these parents matter somewhat more...than the researchers claimed."[44] In "denying this probability" they are capitulating to "heterosexist ideology" which is "apt to prove counterproductive in the long run."[45]

An aside: gender confusion

Gender confusion seems to be rife, with daughters of lesbian mothers more likely to value and exhibit male sex-typed traits, and sons more female-valued traits.[46] Studies are apt to dismiss significant statistical differences in sex-typed behaviour between the children of lesbians and heterosexuals, as 'normal' or unremarkable. Philip Belcastro and colleagues draw attention to the work of B. Hoeffer, who found that twice as many boys of heterosexual mothers scored sex-type masculine than boys of lesbian mothers, and 40 per cent of the boys of lesbian mothers scored sex-type feminine as opposed to no boys of heterosexual mothers. Omitted from Hoeffer's published version of the original dissertation were the statistically significant results that 50 per cent of the girls of lesbian mothers also scored as sex-type masculine compared to no girls of heterosexual mothers and that girls of lesbian mothers had higher scores on male-valued traits than girls of heterosexual mothers (and conversely for female-valued traits); likewise, the sons of lesbians had higher scores on female-valued traits than the sons of heterosexual mothers.[47]

Growing-up gay

Surveys of post-adolescent offspring show large proportions with a homosexual life-style. One study, of 48 offspring of gay parents aged between 14 and 33, found that about eight per cent of the children were themselves gay or lesbian.[48] Another reported that 33 per cent of boys and eight per cent of girls of homosexual fathers were themselves homosexual, although the sample was very small at 19.[49] Another recent study of the sexual orientation of 75 adult sons of gay fathers, gave nine per cent as gay or bisexual, or a rate "several times higher than that suggested by the population based surveys".[50] In a 1989 survey of women once married to practising homosexual men, nearly 12 per cent reported homosexual behaviour in their older children, and a third mentioned that their children had problems in relationships with the opposite sex.[51]

In a study of 5,182 randomly obtained adults from six US cities, 17 answered questionnaires indicating that they had a homosexual parent. These 17 disproportionately reported sexual relations with parents, relatives and other caretakers, as well as gender dissatisfaction, and that their first sexual experience was homosexual.[52] At least six of the 17 (or 35 per cent) became homosexual. As critics of the homosexual movement, Paul and Kirk Cameron defend the use of this small sample, given that – elsewhere – "a cursory examination of the children of 14 rather casually obtained transsexuals/homosexuals is being employed not only as 'a classic' effort, but somehow also as a definitive study... We make no claims that ours is 'representative' of homosexual parenting – but others have been permitted to make such claims with considerably less data."[53]

It is usual to claim that figures for homosexual outcomes are 'within the normal range of variability in the population.' Charlotte J. Patterson categorically states how "...development of gender identity, of gender role behaviour, and of sexual preference...was found in every study to fall within normal bounds...no evidence has been found for significant disturbances of any kind in the development of sexual identity among these individuals."[54] Susan Golombok and Fiona Tasker observe how one "...of the most commonly voiced assumptions about lesbian families is that the children will themselves grow up to be lesbian or gay, an outcome which is generally considered to be undesirable by those involved in decision making in courts of law,"[55] and refer, in refutation back to Patterson's article where "8 per cent of young adults raised by lesbian mothers reported a sexual orientation towards partners of the same sex, which is consistent with general population norms."[56]

This is not consistent, unless assertions made by Kinsey are believed – that 10 per cent of the population is homosexual. In reality according to the largest and most detailed study to date, only 0.3 per cent of British men have only ever had male sex partners, 3.6 per cent of men have had same sex genital contact in their life, 1.4 per cent in the past five years and 1.1 per cent have had a homosexual partner in the last year. Only 0.1 per cent of women have had exclusively female sexual partners and 1.8 per cent has had a female sexual partner in their lifetime.[57] Similarly, an omnibus survey by the Office of National Statistics found that two per cent of men had had homosexual intercourse with a man at some time in their life, but a half of this group had also had intercourse with a woman.[58] An official US study found that 5.5 per cent of Americans had had homosexual intercourse, but that only 0.6 per cent were exclusively homosexual.[59] Figures of between eight to 24 per cent or more (the percentage grows with age)[60] are given as homosexual for the children of homosexuals. These statistics are at least four or five times higher than for the general population, where men are concerned. It seems reasonable to conclude that homosexual parents are associated disproportionately with homosexual children.

It has been said that "it is difficult to conceive of a credible theory of sexual development that would not expect the children of lesbigay [sic] parents to display a somewhat higher incidence of homoerotic desire, behaviour and identity than children of heterosexual parents."[61]

Possible causes of same-sex attraction

If it were true that there was any genetic or biological basis or predisposition for homosexuality, a greater frequency among the children of homosexuals would be expected. One of the studies referred to above, involving 75 adult sons of gay fathers, found that there was no association between a son's sexual orientation and years with their father, the frequency of contact, the acceptance of their fathers' gay identity, or the quality of the father/son relationships.[62] This might imply that genes are at work. However, women reared by lesbians are as likely or more likely than men reared by lesbians to become homosexual although lesbians are far less prevalent than homosexual men in the general population. This suggests that a homosexual same-sex parent has a greater influence on sexual preference than a homosexual opposite-sex parent. This raises matters of culture, or environmental pressures, as well as genetics in the creation of sexual identity and sexual preference. There are indications that girls may worry more than boys about becoming homosexual as the result of having a lesbian mother. Perhaps boys are more able to distance themselves in being less identified with their mother and less interested in relationships.

It is usually implied that sexual preference is established by early or mid childhood, and is unchangeable, so that youngsters need help in 'coming out' to express a fixed identity over which no one has any control. Thus as one former MP turned novelist has suggested, a male homosexual in a "lavender marriage" is "denying his true nature to the rest of the world", as well as "making it more difficult for those who want to avoid such deception." In turn someone owning early homosexual adventures, while disclaiming any present homosexual inclinations is implying that "gay love is a teenage folly, readily corrected, akin to acne or binge drinking."[63] But, disappointing as it may seem to Edwina Currie, over a half of all men and two thirds of women who report having had a same-gender partner in their lifetime have only had one and so have never repeated the experience.[64]

Identical (monozygotic) twins have the same genes but do not necessarily share the same orientation and non-identical (fraternal twins) show higher rates of concordance than ordinary brothers and sisters (although they have no greater genetic similarity). Individuals may switch their sexual identities at various points in their lives. This also suggests cultural and social influences as well as biological factors.[65] A large-scale survey of sexual orientation in US adolescents (34,706), found that only a half of those reporting a homosexual or bisexual orientation at 12, claimed the same at 18 (1.6 per cent to 0.8 per cent).[66] It is often claimed that 'sexual orientation is fixed at 16',[67] but the Sigma study showed that, among other things, the average age at first anal intercourse for men was 20.9 years.[68] Suggesting that many people do not become aware of their homosexuality until adulthood, one researcher reported how nearly a third of the men and nearly three-quarters of the women in his study were unaware of their homosexuality when they married.[69]

Activists seem to want to turn homosexuality into a commitment and destiny that locks people into what may only be a passing state in their emotional and sexual development. Bisexuality "in early adulthood may represent a transitional phase in which preferences are tested through experimentation with different lifestyles and relationships."[70] The majority of those who continue to engage in homosexual activity as adults also engage in heterosexual activity, being generally promiscuous. Homosexuality is not distributed in the population either randomly or uniformly like left-handedness or intelligence.[71] The incidence varies widely between different religious groups and the incidence of sexual relations with partners of the same sex is far greater in urban compared to rural areas. This may be owed to fewer sanctions and more suggestions and opportunities for same-gender sexual interest and behaviour.[72] The processes at work may perhaps be illustrated by a report of a 25 year old man who "...had his first sexual experience when he was 13 years old. It was arranged by his lesbian mother with an older gay man. After...his imagery and interpersonal sexual experience were exclusively homosexual."[73] The majority of lesbians in Golombok and colleagues' initial study claimed that they had no preference as to whether their children would be homosexual or heterosexual.[74] In this way permission to become homosexual is internalised, [75] just as drug taking is for the children of a drug-using parent who asserts that this is their 'choice.' Indeed children may feel that they are disappointing a parent or letting them down if they *do not* become homosexual:

> "At first, I thought my mom would love me more if I was gay. But when we talked about it, she said she'd love me the same whatever I was... My mom was telling me the other day that my grandma and grandpa were saying they were worried about me turning out gay. My mom told them it was going to be my choice."[76]

Elsewhere, a bisexual woman recounts how:

> "I became the school dyke... I wasn't interested in boys at all... I kept trying to proselytize to little girls, saying it's all right to be gay. People got a bit annoyed with me over that... I've been going out with a boy...and I've slept with a couple of women since then. It's good fun... I have experimented sexually, and my parents have created a supportive environment for that... My Mum was more supportive when I had a girlfriend than when I went out with boys".[77]

Identity may follow behaviour, as with a study of women who reported no homosexual interests or experiences up to 30, but came to identify themselves as bisexual, following homosexual acts as part of partner-swapping.[78] This tends to be underlined by the way in which homosexual victimisation frequently leads to the victim becoming homosexual, with learning through experience an important avenue into sexual preference. Research on outcomes for sexually abused young males, found that early homosexual contact with an adult was highly related to homosexual outcomes. Around a half who reported childhood sexual experience with an older man, later identified themselves as homosexual or were involved in homosexual activity.[79] At one point, Susan Golombok and Fiona Tasker admit how, from a social learning perspective:

"...it could be expected that different patterns of reinforcement may be operating in homosexual than in heterosexual families such that young people in lesbian and gay families would be less likely to be discouraged from engaging in non conventional sex-typed behaviour or from embarking upon lesbian or gay relationships. Whereas contemporary social learning theorists are less likely than classical social learning theorists to emphasize the importance of the same-sex parent as a role model, it could be argued that by virtue of their nontraditional family, the sons and daughters of lesbian mothers and gay fathers may hold less rigid stereotypes about what constitutes acceptable male and female behaviour than their peers in heterosexual families, and may be more open to nonconventional gender-role behaviour, or to involvement in lesbian and gay relationships themselves."[80]

Children in difficulties

It is especially girl children of lesbian mothers who tend to endorse the possibility of being either homosexual or heterosexual. Depending upon their experiences they might turn either way, or change their sexual orientation. Most young adults with a homosexual or bisexual parent are reported as going through a period when they question their own sexuality, even given that awareness of the parent's same-sex relationships may give rise to feelings of discomfort and distaste. Adolescent boys may experience these difficulties in terms of threats to masculinity or self-esteem.[81] Accounts of an anti-male ethos in lesbian environments permeate the literature:

"A few months after Deana left, my mother started to see another woman, but that didn't last...then she got involved with another woman...she'd be violent toward my mother...my mom went back to University and she started to get political. Then my mom was dismissed from her job because she was a lesbian, and after that she started to go on marches and to women's groups...there were some women in these groups who objected to men altogether, and I couldn't cope with that. There was one woman who was working on my mom's case, and she went at me one time because I was male

– and I was only twelve or thirteen then... I didn't really talk about my mother to anybody." (Male aged 19)

"...I couldn't figure out my own sexuality, because I was having sex with people of both sexes...my mother was involved in the radical feminist lesbian movement in Washington, D.C....[and so] I was being exposed to damaging experiences... I was twelve at the time – would be left with other lesbians who said horrible things to us. I distinctly remember a woman telling me, 'You are a most despicable thing on earth because you are nothing but a future man'...for me, this kind of hatred ruined my life." (Male aged 27)

"As time went on, my mother and Linda were more and more separatist... When I started fourth grade in our local public school, they notified the principal and the teachers that they were lesbians... I went back to public school for junior high. By then, things were very bad at home... I was discouraged from having male friends, and any female friends were made aware that I lived in a lesbian household before I could have them over... I experienced separatism as a constant level of anger and negativity...men were called mutants, straight women were considered disowned sisters who wasted woman-energy on men, and other lesbians were sometimes accused of being government spies sent to infiltrate and undermine the community. Anyone who was not like us was evil..."(Female aged 25)[82]

Clearly, not only is one of the sexes absent from lesbian homes, but the children's understanding of relationships and sexuality is viewed daily from a homosexual perspective. Hypersexualisation is associated with homosexuality, both in terms of promiscuity and sexuality as the focus of identity and self-worth.

What's wrong with gay children?

Does it matter if the children are "more open to nonconventional gender-role behaviour, or to involvement in lesbian and gay relationships themselves"?[83] What is amiss with steering children towards homosexuality? What is wrong with children seeing, or even participating in, displays of homosexual activities, compared with displays of affection between married heterosexual parents? At the same time as exponents of homosexual parenting claim that the high proportion of homosexual children of homosexual parents reflects population norms, this is also held as a positive indication of how these youngsters are "better informed about lesbian and gay lifestyles and know about lesbian and gay possibilities at an earlier age."[84] Having a lesbian mother

> "appeared to widen the adolescent's view of what constituted acceptable sexual behaviour to include same-gender sexual relationships... In contrast, participants from heterosexual single-parent backgrounds did not consider same-gender sexual relationships a possibility and their repertoires of sexual relationship options were generally limited to heterosexual relationships."[85]

Moreover, greater prevalence of homosexual parenting with its greater production of homosexual offspring, is welcomed as part of a changing social climate which will influence the acceptance and growth of same-gender relationships. This makes it "conceivable...that children born at the present time to heterosexual parents who are accepting of lesbian and gay relationships will be just as open to same-sex exploration in adulthood as their counterparts from lesbian families are today." [86]

Reports of life satisfaction have long been considered an important guide to psychological and social well-being. In a major US survey,[87] 60.9 per cent of heterosexuals compared to 46.4 per cent of homosexuals said that they were "extremely" or "very happy" with their life over the past 12 months. In turn, 11.5 per cent of heterosexuals compared to 20 per cent of homosexuals said that they were "fairly unhappy" or "unhappy most of the time". In the same study, 67.5 per cent of the married, compared to 39.6 per cent of the divorced reported being happy with their personal lives, and 8.7 per cent of the married and 21.4 per cent of the divorced reported being unhappy with their personal lives. In turn,

51.2 per cent of those below the poverty line compared to 59.5 per cent of the economically advantaged reported being happy with their lives, while 19.4 per cent of the 'poor' and 13.1 per cent of the 'rich' reported unhappiness. Homosexuals thus rated their lives less happy than the married, and about as unhappy as the divorced and the impoverished.

Homosexuals also suffer disproportionately from a range of morbid conditions compared to heterosexuals, particularly sexually transmitted diseases, like gonorrhoea, syphilis, hepatitis A and B, anorectal warts and AIDS (in the latest report, to June 2001, 13,589 cases of HIV infection in men were due to homosexual intercourse out of a total of 19,725, or 69 per cent, and in the year to June 1997, 871 men died of AIDS).[88] Homosexual practices frequently result in physical injuries, not least to the rectum.[89] Homosexuals are also disproportionately involved in alcohol and substance abuse.[90]

The effect on future families

As well as the effect of homosexual parenting on children's sexual orientation, there are questions about the role of parental behaviour, attitudes and activities on heterosexual conduct. It is now well known that family behaviour tends to be intergenerational. The consequences for future family formation have been identified as the strongest, and perhaps the most important, outcomes when it comes to the effect of family structure on behaviour.[91] The children of divorce or single motherhood are proportionally far more likely to repeat cycles of divorce and non-marriage than those born to married couples who stay in intact families. As seen in our National Survey of Sexual Attitudes and Lifestyles, young women are more likely to become teenage mothers if they had lived with only one parent as a child.[92] The National Survey of Family Growth (involving 7,969 US women aged 15-44 years), found that women who spent time with a lone-parent were 111 per cent more likely to have teenage births, 164 per cent more likely to have premarital births and 92 per cent more likely to have failed marriages than daughters who grew up in two-parent homes.[93] In Britain, young women whose parents' marriages had broken down by the time they were 16 have been found to be more likely to cohabit in their teens, to have a child by 20, and to have extra-marital births. These findings were altered little if at all by the introduction of background controls for childhood hardship, social group and earlier behaviour.[94] Almost double the number of young men in the British Child Development Study who experienced parental divorce dissolved their own marriage by their early 30s compared to those whose parents had stayed together (33 per cent against 18 per cent).[95] The earlier National Survey of Health and Development, which addressed the same questions, with a cohort of children born in 1946, also found that only two factors were directly and independently related to the probability of marriage breakdown in adulthood – parental divorce and psychological well-being at age 15.[96]

Such findings are more or less worldwide. In the Utrecht Study of Adolescent Development,[97] children of divorced or other lone-parents more often gave birth earlier and outside marriage, got married or cohabited earlier, had more conflict with partners, and got divorced more often. Similarly, in the New Zealand Christchurch longitudinal sample of children born in 1977, 20 per cent of children experienced family break-up in their first five years if their mother had experienced parental separation before 16, compared to just over 12 per cent of children whose mothers were reared in stable two-parent families.[98] From the US longitudinal data of the National Survey of Families and Households, it is estimated that parental divorce increases the odds of disruption for women within the first five years of marriage by 70 per cent.[99] In the Study of Marriage over the Life Course, the percentage of marriages breaking down between 1980 and 1992 was 11 per cent in the first marriage for those where neither spouse's parents divorced.[100] When wives experienced parental divorce, the odds of divorce increased by half and when both spouses experienced parental divorce, the odds nearly tripled.

It is likely that parental role models, lack of parental input and supervision – or a socialisation effect, plus effects on attitudes and values about relationships[101] – provide explanations. [102] The knock-on effect of parental behaviour on relationships in the following generation may also reflect a lack of understanding, or confidence in the making, of stable, intimate ties. Parents who divorce may set an example about the desirability or necessity of marriage, so that it becomes downgraded or marginalized for the children. When parents have more favourable or accepting attitudes to divorce and separation, or less favourable attitudes to marriage, both may be transmitted to their children and lead to higher rates of both cohabitation and divorce.[103]

All this seems even more likely to be the case with homosexual parents and their children. In G.A. Javaid's New York City study of teenage children of lesbian mothers, 27 per cent – versus 11 per cent of the children of divorced heterosexual mothers – had reservations regarding future marriage and children.[104] Elsewhere, children of homosexual parents are seen to be less frequently married than their peers, and more rejecting of marriage and having children.[105] If many children of homosexuals either seem to become single mothers or want to avoid marriage and children, then a troubled childhood is more likely to result in adults who are less able or willing to contribute to society. In the Fiona Tasker and Susan Golombok study, 38 per cent of the lesbians' daughters compared to 11 per cent of the heterosexuals' daughters reported having had 10 or more sexual relationships. In turn, 64 per cent of the lesbian children had ever cohabited compared to 60 per cent of the heterosexuals – reflecting the generally high rates of cohabitational experience in present day society. But whereas all the children of heterosexuals who had ever cohabited had done so only once, 20 per cent of the lesbians' children had cohabited at least twice.[106] Facing up to and coping with a child's marriage can be difficult for lesbians if a textbook on lesbian parenting is anything to go by. It seems that "weddings can bring up a host of charged emotions", because:

> "For one thing, you can't legally marry your partner. And given the patriarchal heritage and practice of marriage as an institution, you might not want to if you could. Happy as you may be for your child, your feelings about the institution of marriage may range from resentment to rage. For some lesbian parents, this may mean not even wanting to attend their child's wedding."[107]

Endnotes:

[1] Golombok S, Spencer, A and Rutter, M, 'Children in Lesbian and Single-Parent Households: Psychosexual and Psychiatric appraisal', *Journal of Child Psychology and Psychiatry,* 24(4), 1983, pages 551-572

[2] That is, an assessment as to what extent the results obtained could be replicated with different investigators.

[3] These are different measures of childhood behaviour in terms of the sex of the child.

[4] Rowe J, Cain H, Hundleby, M and Keane, A, *Long-Term Foster Care,* Batsford Academic and Educational in association with British Agencies for Adoption and Fostering London, 1984, pages 82-83

[5] *Ibid,* pages 30, 86, 203

[6] Thorpe, R, *The Social and Psychological Situation of the Long-Term Foster Child with Regard to His Natural Parents,* Unpublished phD thesis, University of Nottingham, 1974 quoted in Rowe J, Cain H, Hundleby, M and Keane, A, *Op cit,* page 84

[7] Campbell, S B, 'Behavior Problems in Preschool Children: A Review of Recent Research', *Journal of Child Psychology and Psychiatry,* 36(1), 1995, pages 113-149

[8] Richman N, Stevenson, J and Graham P J, *Pre-school to School: a Behavioural Study,* Academic Press, London, 1982, page 31

[9] Meltzer, H et al, *The Mental Health of Children and Adolescents in Great Britain,* Office for National Statistics, The Stationery Office, London, 2000, pages 26, 27, 33

[10] Kirkpatrick M, Smith, C and Roy, R, 'Lesbian Mothers and their Children: A Comparative Survey', *American Journal of Orthopsychiatry,* 51(3), 1981, pages 545-551

[11] Tasker, F and Golombok, S, 'Adults Raised as Children in Lesbian Families', *Op cit,* pages 203-215
Golombok S, Spencer, A and Rutter, M, *Op cit,* page 558 and see Tasker, F and Golombok, S, *Growing Up in a Lesbian Family,* The Guilford Press, London, 1997

[12] Cameron, P, 'Homosexual Parents: Testing "Common Sense" – a Literature Review Emphasizing the Golombok and Tasker Longitudinal Study of Lesbians' Children', *Op cit,* page 306

[13] *Ibid,* pages 286-287

[14] Campbell, S B, *Op cit,* page 119

[15]   Tasker, F and Golombok, S, *Growing Up in a Lesbian Family*, *Op cit*, Table 7.4, page 141

[16]   Tasker, F and Golombok, S, 'Adults Raised as Children in Lesbian Families', *Op cit*, pages 208-209

[17]   *Ibid*, page 207

[18]   *Ibid*, pages 203-215

[19]   *Ibid*, page 211

[20]   *Ibid*, pages 209-210

[21]   Tasker, F and Golombok, S, *Growing Up in a Lesbian Family*, *Op cit*, page 67

[22]   Pennington, S B, 'Children of Lesbian Mothers', in Bozett, F W (Ed.) *Gay and Lesbian Parents*, Praeger, New York, 1987, pages 62-63

[23]   *Ibid*, page 62

[24]   Rae, G, '"Therapy with a Lesbian Stepfamily with an Electively Mute Child": A Comment', *Journal of Family Psychotherapy*, 6(1), 1995, pages 15-20

[25]   Javaid, G A, 'The Children of Homosexual and Heterosexual Single Mothers', *Child Psychiatry and Human Development*, 23(4), Summer 1993, page 243

[26]   Pennington, S B, *Op cit*, page 63

[27]   O'Connell, A, 'Voices from the Heart: The Developmental Impact of a Mother's Lesbianism on her Adolescent Children', in Laird J (Ed.) *Op cit*, pages 275, 270, 271

[28]   Cramer, D, 'Gay Parents and Their Children: A Review of Research and Practical Implications', *Journal of Counseling and Development*, 64, 1986, pages 504-507; and
Riddle, D I, de Lourdes Arguelles, M, 'Children of Gay Parents: Homophobia's Victims' in Stuart, I R and Abt, L E, (Eds.) *Children of Separation and Divorce*, Van Nostrand Reinhold Company, New York, 1981, pages 174-187

[29]   Wyers, N L, 'Homosexuality in the Family: Lesbian and Gay Spouses', *Social Work*, 32(2), 1987, pages 143-148

[30]   Lewis, K G, 'Children of Lesbians: their Point of View', *Social Work*, 25(4), 1980, pages 198, 200

[31]   Rafkin, L, *Different Mothers: Sons and Daughters of Lesbians Talk about their Lives*, Cleis Press, Pittsburgh, 1990

[32]   *Ibid*, pages 13-15

[33]   Sarantakos, S, 'Children in Three Contexts: Family, Education and Social Development', *Children Australia*, 21(3), 1996, pages 23-31

34 *Ibid*, page 25

35 *Ibid*, page 26

36 Pennington, S B, *Op cit*, page 61

37 Massow, I, 'Gay Tories, that's one thing. But gay dads?', *The Observer*, 31 October 1999

38 Golombok, S and Tasker, F, 'Do Parents Influence the Sexual Orientation of Their Children? Findings From a Longitudinal Study of Lesbian Families', *Developmental Psychology*, 32(1), 1996, pages 3-11

39 Tasker, F and Golombok, S, *Growing Up in a Lesbian Family*, *Op cit*, page 124, Table 6.5

40 Golombok, S and Tasker, F, 'Do Parents Influence the Sexual Orientation of Their Children? Findings From a Longitudinal Study of Lesbian Families', *Op cit*, page 7

41 O'Connell, A, *Op cit*, page 272

42 Stonewall, *Factsheets 5- Equal as Parents*, as at 11 February 2000

43 Stacey, J and Biblarz, T J, *Op cit*, page 163

44 *Ibid*, page 167

45 *Ibid*, page 178

46 Green, R et al 'Lesbian Mothers and their Children: A Comparison with Solo Parent Heterosexual Mothers and Their Children', *Archives of Sexual Behaviour*, 15, 1986, pages 167-183; and
Hoeffer, B 'Lesbian and Heterosexual Single Mothers' Influence of Their Children's Acquisition of Sex-Role Traits and Behavior', Dissertation, University of California (Ann Arbor: UMI) 1979 cited in Belcastro, P et al, *Op cit*, pages 117-118

47 Hoeffer, B 'Children's Acquisition of Sex-Role Behavior', *American Journal of Orthopsychiatry*, 51, 1981, pages 536-543; and Hoeffer, B 'Lesbian and Heterosexual Single Mothers' Influence of Their Children's Acquisition of Sex-Role Traits and Behavior', *Op cit*, pages 111-112

48 Miller, B, 'Gay Fathers and Their Children', *The Family Coordinator*, 28, 1979, pages 544-552

49 Gottman, J S, 'Children of Gay and Lesbian Parents', in Bozett, F W and Sussman, M B (Eds.) *Homosexuality and Family Relations*, The Haworth Press, New York, 1990, page 183

50 Bailey J M, Bobrow D, Wolfe, M and Mikach, S, 'Sexual Orientation of Adult Sons of Gay Fathers', *Developmental Psychology*, 31(1), 1995, pages 124-129

51 Hays, D and Samuels, A, 'Heterosexual Women's Perceptions of Their Marriages to Bisexual or Homosexual Men' in Bozett F W (Ed.) *Homosexual-*

ity and the Family, The Haworth Press, New York, 1989, pages 81, 96, 97

52   Cameron, P and Cameron, K, 'Homosexual Parents', *Op cit*, pages 757-776. Five of them (or 29 per cent), reported sex with the homosexual parent, and this accounted for 18 per cent of the sexual interactions between children and parents or step-parents in the entire sample (on the assumption that all the other parent/child sexual interactions were heterosexual), although children raised by homosexuals accounted for less than 0.4 per cent of the sample. Having a homosexual parent seemed to increase the risk of incest with a parent by a factor of about 50.

53   *Ibid*, page 774.
This refers to the analysis by Bozett, F W, 'Children of Gay Fathers', in Bozett, F W (Ed.) *Gay and Lesbian Parents*, *Op cit*, pages 46-48 of Green, R, 'Sexual Identity of 37 Children Raised by Homosexual or Transsexual Parents', *American Journal of Psychiatry*, 135(6), 1978, pages 692-697. Green's article is also used by Patterson, C J, in 'Children of Lesbian and Gay Parents', *Op cit*, pages 1031, 1033

54   Patterson, C J, 'Children of Lesbian and Gay Parents', *Op cit*, pages 1031-1032

55   Golombok, S and Tasker, F, 'Children in Lesbian and Gay Families: Theories and Evidence', *Op cit*, page 80

56   *Ibid*, page 81 citing Patterson, C J, 'Children of Lesbian and Gay Parents', *Op cit*, pages 1031-1032. Patterson is actually reviewing Miller, B, *Op cit*, pages 546-547

57   Wellings, K, et al, *Op cit*, pages 209, 188 (with Table 5.4), 217. The new National Survey of Sexual Attitudes and Lifestyles was published at the time of going to press, but its sample size is smaller, 11,000, and it excludes the age range 45-59, used in the 1990 survey. The proportion of exclusively homosexual men in the survey does not appear to have been published to date. Johnson, A M et al, 'Sexual Behaviour in Britain: Partnerships, Practices and HIV Risk Behaviours', *The Lancet*, 358, December 2001, pages 1835-1841.

58   House of Lords, Hansard, 27 November 1997, col. 137 wa

59   Smith, T W, *Adult Sexual Behaviour in 1989: Number of Partners, Frequency and Risk*. GSS Topical report No. 18, NORC, University of Chicago, 1990, page 19

60   Hays, D and Samuels, A, *Op cit*, pages 81-100;
Bozett, F W, 'Children of Gay Fathers', in Bozett, F W (Ed.), *Gay and Lesbian Parents*, *Op cit*, page 47;

Miller, B, *Op cit*, pages 544-552
Tasker and Golombok found that six of the 25 children in their study had a homosexual relationship as a young adult. This is 24 per cent of those in the study. Tasker, F and Golombok, S, 'Adults Raised as Children in Lesbian Families', *Op cit*, page 210

[61] Stacey, J and Biblarz, T J, *Op cit*, page 163

[62] Bailey J M, Bobrow D, Wolfe, M and Mikach, S, *Op cit*, pages 126-127

[63] Currie, E, 'Straying from the Straight and Narrow', *The Times*, 25 March 2000

[64] Johnson, A M et al, *Sexual Attitudes and Lifestyles*, Blackwell Scientific Publications, Oxford, 1994, pages 212-213. The new National Survey of Sexual Attitudes and Lifestyles was published at the time of going to press. The papers published to date do not give such comprehensive statistics on the number of homosexual partners. Johnson, A M et al, 'Sexual Behaviour in Britain: Partnerships, Practices and HIV Risk Behaviours', *The Lancet*, 358, December 2001, pages 1835-1841.

[65] Hubbard, R and Wald, E, *Exploding the Gene Myth*, Beacon Press, Boston, 1993, page 97;
Eckert E D, Bouchard T J, Boulen, J and Heston, L L, 'Homosexuality in Monozygotic Twins Reared Apart', *British Journal of Psychiatry*, 148, 1986, pages 421-425; and
Laumann E O, Gagnon J H, Michael, R T and Michaels, S, *The Social Organisation of Sexuality: Sexual Practices in the United States*, The University of Chicago Press, 1994, pages 308-309

[66] Remafedi G, Resnick M, Blum, R, and Harris, L, 'Demography of Sexual Orientation in Adolescents', *Pediatrics*, 89(4), 1992, pages 714-721

[67] See for example, *Euan Sutherland v UK* (Application 25186/94) Report of the Commission, 1 July 1997, para 64

[68] Weatherburn, P et al, *Op cit*, page 13

[69] Wyers, N, *Op cit*, pages 143-148

[70] Johnson, A M et al, *Op cit*, page 204

[71] Laumann E O, Gagnon J H, Michael, R T and Michaels, S, *Op cit*, page 307

[72] *Ibid*, pages 308, 511-517, 534-537

[73] Schwarz, M F and Masters, W H, 'The Masters and Johnson Treatment Program for Dissatisfied Homosexual Men', *American Journal of Psychiatry*, 141(2), 1984, page 173

[74] Golombok S, Spencer, A and Rutter, M, *Op cit*, page 561

[75] Tasker, F L and Golombok, S, *Growing up in a Lesbian family*, *Op cit*, pages 17, 117

[76]   Rafkin, L, *Op cit*, page 81
[77]   Saffron, L, *What About the Children? Sons and Daughters of Lesbian and Gay Parents talk about their Lives*, Cassell, London, 1996, pages 137-138
[78]   Dixon, J K, 'The Commencement of Bisexual Activity in Swinging Married Women Over Age Thirty', *Journal of Sex Research* 20(1), 1984, pages 71-90
[79]   Johnson, R L and Shrier, D K, 'Sexual Victimisation of Boys: Experience at an Adolescent Medicine Clinic', *Journal of Adolescent Health Care*, 6, 1985, pages 372-376; supported by
       Van Wyk, P H and Geist, C S, 'Psychosocial Development of Heterosexual, Bisexual, and Homosexual Behaviour', *Archives of Sexual Behaviour*, 13(6), 1984, pages 505-544
[80]   Golombok, S and Tasker, F, 'Children in Lesbian and Gay Families: Theories and Evidence', *Op cit*, page 79
[81]   Paul, J P, 'Growing Up with a Gay, Lesbian, or Bisexual Parent: An Exploratory Study of Experiences and Perceptions', Dissertation, University of California, Berkeley (Ann Arbor: UMI), 1986. Cited Belcastro et al, *Op cit*, page 108;
       Lewis, K G, *Op cit*, pages 198-203;
       Kirkpatrick, M, 'Clinical Implications of Lesbian Mother Studies', *Journal of Homosexuality* 14(1-2), 1987, pages 201-211
[82]   Rafkin, L, *Op cit*, pages 145-147, 110-112, 54-58
[83]   Golombok, S and Tasker, F, 'Children in Lesbian and Gay Families: Theories and Evidence', *Op cit*, page 79
[84]   Golombok, S and Tasker, F, 'Do Parents Influence the Sexual Orientation of Their Children? Findings From a Longitudinal Study of Lesbian Families', *Op cit*, page 10
[85]   Tasker, F and Golombok, S, 'Adults Raised as Children in Lesbian Families', *Op cit*, page 212
[86]   Golombok, S and Tasker, F, 'Do Parents Influence the Sexual Orientation of Their Children? Findings From a Longitudinal Study of Lesbian Families', *Op cit*, page 10
[87]   Laumann E O, Gagnon J H, Michael, R T and Michaels, S, *Op cit*, page 351 with Table 10.2A and Table 10.4
[88]   Communicable Disease Report, Public Health Laboratory Service, 9(18), 30 April 1999, pages 156-157;
       Sexually Transmitted Infections Still on the Increase, Press Release, Public Health Laboratory Service, 27 July 2001;
       Communicable Disease Report, Public Health Laboratory Service, 7(42), 17

October 1997, page 373;
AIDS/HIV Quarterly Surveillance Tables, Public Health Laboratory Service
AIDS Centre, and the Scottish Centre for Infection and Environmental
Health, No. 51:01/2, July 2001, Table 1; and Communicable Disease Report,
Public Health Laboratory Service AIDS and STD Centre, Scottish Centre for
Infection and Environmental Health et al, 7(30), July 1997, Table 1. (Separate
figures for each year are no longer published.)

[89] Coplan, P M et al 'Human Immunodeficiency Virus Infection in Mexico City',
American Journal of Epidemiology, 144(9), 1996, pages 817-827; Sohn, N and
Robilotti, J G, 'The Gay Bowel Syndrome', *American Journal of Gastroen-
terology*, 67(5), 1977, pages 478-484; Frisch, M et al 'Sexually Transmitted
Infection as a Cause of Anal Cancer', New England Journal of Medicine,
337(19), 1997, pages 1350-1358

[90] Skinner, W F, 'The Prevalence and Demographic Predictors of Illicit and Licit
Drug Use among Lesbians and Gay Men', *American Journal of Public
Health*, 84 (8), 1994, pages 1307-1310

[91] For example, from the American PSID (Panel Study of Income Dynamics)
sample, Sara McLanahan calculated that living with a lone mother at age 16
increases a daughter's risk of becoming a female head of household during
the next year by 72 per cent for whites and 100 per cent for blacks. Exposure
at any time during adolescence increases the risk to 137 per cent for whites.
Differences in the incomes of one- and two-parent families only seem to be
related to 25 per cent of the difference in offspring behaviours.
McLanahan, S, 'Family Structure and Dependency: Early Transitions to
Female Household Headship', *Demography*, 25(1), 1988, pages 1-16

[92] Wellings, K, *The National Survey of Sexual Attitudes and Lifestyles:
Teenage Pregnancy*, Research results, No. 4, Economic and Social Research
Council, June 1997

[93] McLanahan, S and Bumpass, L, "Intergenerational Consequences of Family
Disruption", *American Journal of Sociology*, 94(1), 1988, pages 130-152

[94] Kiernan, K E, 'The Impact of Family Disruption in Childhood on Transitions
Made in Young Adult Life', *Population Studies 46*, 1992, pages 213-234

[95] Kiernan, K, *The Legacy of Parental Divorce: Social, economic and demographic experiences in adulthood*, CASE paper 1, Centre for Analysis of
Social Exclusion, London School of Economics, 1997, pages 30-31

[96] *Ibid* and confirmed by the later Economic and Social Research Council's
(ESRC) sample. Wertheimer, A and McRae, S, *Family and Household
Change in Britain; A Summary of findings from projects in the ESRC*

Population and Household Change Programme, Centre for Family and Household Research Oxford, 1999

[97] Spruijt, E and De Goede, M, 'Changing Family Structures and Adolescent Well-being in the Netherlands', *International Journal of Law, Policy and the Family*, 10, 1996, pages 1-16

[98] Fergusson, D M, 'Family Formation, Dissolution and Reformation', *Proceedings of the SSRFC Symposium: New Zealand Families in the Eighties and Nineties*, Canterbury University, 20, November 1987, page 29

[99] Bumpass L L, Martin, T C and Sweet, J A, 'The Impact of Family Background and Early Marital Factors on Marital Disruption', *Journal of Family Issues*, 12(1), 1991, pages 22-42

[100] Amato, P R, 'Explaining the Intergenerational Transmission of Divorce', *Journal of Marriage and the Family*, 58, 1996, pages 628-640

[101] Axinn, W G and Thornton A, 'The Relationship between Cohabitation and Divorce: Selectivity or Casual Influence?' *Demography* 29(3), 1992, pages 357-374

[102] Thornton, A and Camburn, D, 'The Influence of the Family on Premarital Sexual Attitudes and Behavior', *Demography*, 24(3), 1987, pages 323-340

[103] In William G. Axinn and Arland Thornton's study, cohabiting by daughters of mothers who agree strongly that married people are happier was only 41 per cent as high as for daughters of those who disagree strongly. Daughters of mothers who would be bothered if they did not marry cohabit at significantly lower rates than daughters of mothers who would not be bothered if they did not marry, and a lesser effect was also observed for sons of mothers who believed married people were happier.
Axinn, W G and Thornton A, *Op cit*, pages 364-365.
In Paul R. Amato and Alan Booth's analysis, parents' 'nontraditional' attitudes and behaviour increased the chances that offspring cohabited either prior to, or instead of, marriage. Moreover, offspring who began cohabiting relationships between 1980 and 1992 were more likely to end these relationships without marrying if parents were reported as 'nontraditional'.
Amato, P R and Booth, A, *A Generation at Risk*, *Op cit*, pages 104, 118

[104] Javaid, G A, *Op cit*, pages 253-248

[105] Rafkin, L, *Op cit*. For example, pages 48, 116, 152, 165, 167

[106] Tasker, F L and Golombok, S, *Growing up in a Lesbian family*, *Op cit*, pages 127, 131

[107] Clunis, D M and Green, G D, *The Lesbian Parenting Book*, Seal Press, Seattle, 1995, page 317

Chapter 4

All else considered?

Where then are the homosexual parents, with parenting not only equivalent to, but better than, that of heterosexual parents? It seems that D.K. Flaks and colleagues found that lesbian mothers of 15 children (average age six) scored significantly higher than heterosexual parents on the Parent Awareness Skills Survey which measures the sensitivity and effectiveness with which a parent responds to typical child-care situations.[1] However, while it might seem that lesbian mothers had more parenting awareness than heterosexual parents, it cannot be concluded that lesbian couples are better at parenting than traditional families. Their opinions regarding children in general in 18 hypothetical situations do not tell us how they rear their own children in real life. Anyway, with further analysis, the difference disappeared, because the fathers in the heterosexual group were pulling down the average. The lesbian couples proved to be superior in their ability to identify the critical issues in child-care situations and to suggest appropriate solutions to the problems they saw. But this highly motivated sample of volunteers were all female, and women talk more than men about hypothetical children. Moreover, the responses were to do with gender differences in verbalising ideas about parenting, rather than fathers being actually less able to handle child-care problems. Scores may have little to do with being an effective parent. However, women generally may be more skilled than men when it comes to providing activities that advance young children's development. This is a matter of sex (or gender), rather than sexual orientation.[2] It need not mean that two female parents are necessarily better than one male and one female, not least because one female will not be related to the child, with all that this entails and because there is a limit to the effects of positive parental input. What fathers contribute to child rearing may be different, but not necessarily inferior, to mothers' contributions – even if not so substantial or critical to early development.

Comparison with married couple families

Stage Three of Sotirios Sarantakos's longitudinal Australian cohabitation study used subsets of a total of 174 children living in married couple families, with heterosexual cohabitees and with homosexual cohabitees (predominantly lesbian) recruited from another project on homosexual couples.[3] It focussed primarily on children's educational and social outcomes and quality of life. The homosexual (and heterosexual cohabitees) were recruited by means of 'snowball' sampling methods, where initial 'cases' were picked up in the context of other studies, and the groups expanded through references to friends, colleagues, neighbours and acquaintances in the same situation. The married sample came from an original study of families in New South Wales. All children of primary school age living with homosexual couples were matched to children living with married and cohabiting, heterosexual couples with the same or similar attributes (education, occupation, employment status, age of child, etc.). In this school based investigation, children of married couples were significantly more likely to do well at school, in academic and social terms, than those of cohabiting heterosexual and homosexual couples. Marriage seemed to provide the best environment for development, in being "more positive, supportive, rich, rewarding, secure and guiding...".[4] The children of the married couples achieved the highest scores in educational assessment and the children of the homosexual couples the lowest, this being most pronounced for language in the areas of verbal and composition skills. The mathematical ability of children of homosexual couples was below the average scores for all students as well as under that for the children of heterosexual cohabitees and married couples. Only in social studies were the three groups roughly commensurate. Insofar as personal adjustment was assessed, the sociability scores for the children of homosexual couples were well below those of the two other groups, with the children of married couples doing best. Married parents controlled and directed their children more than parents in the other two groups. Children of homosexual cohabitees enjoyed the greatest autonomy, followed by children of cohabiting heterosexual couples.

Many children of heterosexual cohabitees had experienced divorce, as had those of homosexual cohabitees – the children of whom were all born in a previous relationship. Again, considering the high break up rate of cohabitations and the prevalence of cohabitation after divorce or parental separation, more children in cohabiting households are likely to have experienced repeated family disruption. By the same token, more children of married couples were likely to be with their two original parents. It is reasonable to assume that parental divorce or separation and step-parenthood may have roles in explaining the difference in educational development of the children in the three contexts. With the married couples and, to a lesser extent, cohabiting heterosexual couples, both parents were likely to be involved with the child's education. With most homosexual couples, only the natural parent of the child provided assistance, personal support and was interested in their school work, as well as carrying responsibility for the control of the child. Susan Golombok and colleagues had also noted the tendency for mothers in lesbian households to have the dominant role in the care of their own children.[5] This situation is paralleled in studies of step-families.[6] Overall, married couples and, to a lesser extent, cohabiting heterosexual couples offered more assistance, more personal support and had more interest in the school work of their children than did homosexual couples, even given that the three groups were matched for the educational status of the parents. Also reflecting the situation found elsewhere with step-relationships – where the natural parent tends to have less interest and investment in their child compared with biological parents in original families[7] – it was far more common for homosexual parents to have no firm expectations concerning the education and future of their child. There was an obvious trend among the children of both homosexual and heterosexual cohabitees to leave school and home as early as possible and set up on their own – another familiar finding for step-children. Other Australian work, the Children in Families Study, also reported significantly less support for children or teenagers in step-families, and their reading ability, self-esteem and self-control was worse than in other family types.[8]

The sperm bank of California

A study purporting to provide an opportunity to examine family functioning among lesbians and heterosexuals which controlled for the effects of biological relatedness, or 'ownness' across families, rated the mental health and social adjustment of children born using the services of the Sperm Bank of California.[9] By definition, this only compares children without two biological parents at home. All the children were related biologically to their mother, and not to any other 'parent' if one was present. This might represent a futuristic departure in the emergence of new 'family forms', or methods of procreation, where women conceive their children via insemination, while having lovers of either sex. It is reminiscent of legends about Amazon societies and exemplifies Anthony Giddens' 'pure relationship'. While this study of homosexual parents and their children involved non-volunteers, there was considerable attrition in the sample. Of the 195 families with children at least five years old, who were considered eligible to participate, only 108 (55.4 per cent) were successfully contacted. Of these, 80 families (74 per cent) agreed to participate, mainly lesbians, so that the final sample consisted of 34 lesbian couple families, 21 lesbian single mothers, 16 heterosexual couple families and nine single heterosexual mothers – well under half the original sample. The children averaged seven years and their families were affluent, with incomes well above the national average. As mentioned earlier, the lesbian biological mothers had completed more years of education than the heterosexual mothers, and the same applied to lesbian non-biological parents, compared to the non-biological fathers.

On average, all the checklists of reports (i.e. from biological mothers, non-biological 'parents', and teachers) agreed that children from all backgrounds were doing well, and that average scores for the internalising, externalising and total behaviour problems scales were significantly below clinical cut-off points. Of the 12 comparisons, seven favoured the children being raised by heterosexuals.[10] Children had more behaviour problems when biological parents reported more parenting distress and more dysfunctional parent/child interactions. The best predictor of teachers' reports of behaviour problems was non-biological parents' parenting stress, and the non-biological parents' reports of dysfunctional parent-child interactions were significantly associated with children's behaviour problems. Non-biological parents' reports of behaviour problems were lower for heterosexuals than for lesbians, in that non-biological 'fathers' tended to describe children in more favourable terms than did non-biological 'mothers'. Among the couples, better relationship adjustment was associated with fewer behaviour problems among the children and both biological and non-biological parents who reported more love in their couple relationships reported children with fewer problems. Again, and consistent with previous findings elsewhere, biological and non-biological parents who reported more conflict also reported that their children had more behaviour problems. As noted, the children were quite young, and "...caution should be exercised in interpreting these data pending replication. Longitudinal studies of representative samples of lesbian and heterosexual parents and their children, including observational as well as questionnaire and interview assessments, would be better able to address questions of change and causal relationships." In turn, "...the inclusion of a comparison group of naturally conceived children would also be beneficial to draw firm conclusions regarding the impact of donor insemination on family processes and children's adjustment."[11]

Controlling for the effects of divorce

Endeavouring to examine the effects of rearing in a female headed family without the confound of parental separation or divorce, a third investigation of Susan Golombok, with colleagues, examined the quality of parent/child relationships and the socio-emotional development of children raised in female headed families from the first year of life.[12] This involved a group of lesbian families (in 15 the mother was alone and in 15 others she lived with her 'partner', 10 of whom had been 'co-mother' from the child's birth), a group of 42 families headed by a single heterosexual mother and a control group of heterosexual two-parent families – all with a child between three and nine years. The assumption is that children reared from infancy without a father would not have been exposed to parental conflict or disrupted family relationships, or experienced the emotional distress (and consequent reduction in parental functioning) common to many lone-mothers. However, the lesbian mothers were, again, a 'volunteer sample'. While it is explained how "...the authors have good access to lesbian families through their longitudinal study of children of lesbian mothers and almost all of those asked to take part agreed to be interviewed", this does not tell us about the criteria for being 'asked'.[13] The 42 families headed by a single heterosexual mother were similarly "selected from a pool of 130 volunteers", obtained through the press. While 41 two-parent heterosexual families were recruited from maternity ward records it is, somewhat mysteriously, reported that the "participation rate was 62%." The demand that the lone lesbian and heterosexual parents were not experiencing hardship, i.e. on state benefits, meant that they had significantly higher socio-economic status than the two-parent families – nearly a third of these were in manual occupations, compared to only three per cent of lesbians. Two-parent families also had more children.

While the samples are hardly comparable, for what it is worth the mothers in both kinds of father-absent families were said to express greater warmth and to have higher levels of interaction with their children: lesbians most of all. The groups did not differ in the level of the mother's emotional involvement with the child or the frequency with which mothers disciplined their children, although disputes between mothers and their children in father-absent families were more severe than in father-present families (as seen elsewhere in comparisons of lone- and two-parent family relationships). Children from father-absent families showed greater 'security of attachment' than children whose father lived with them, although children in father-absent families perceived themselves as less cognitively and physically competent. (Adverse effects of father-absence on various aspects of cognitive functioning, intellectual competence and academic achievement, particularly for boys, have been repeatedly recorded in the literature.[14]) They were no more likely to develop emotional or behaviour problems than children from father-present homes. All apparently suggest " ..the absence of a father from birth or infancy, in itself, does not have negative implications for children's psychological adjustment."[15] However, these findings run counter to what is known about the outcomes for children in father-absent families resulting from divorce (or single motherhood).[16]

While the children studied had not been exposed to parental conflict, separation from a parent with whom they had shared their daily life (and so a mother's emotional distress), or economic hardship, the researchers themselves remind us how "...the recruitment of volunteer lesbian and single heterosexual mothers may have produced biased samples, with mothers whose children were experiencing problems possibly being less likely to take part."[17] It is also recognised how data from general population samples would be necessary to definitively answer questions relating to the effects of father absence from birth on children's development. The researchers also emphasize how, to assess the importance, or otherwise, of a second parent and, particularly, a father, it would be necessary to study children raised by single-heterosexual mothers from birth, presumably conceived using donated semen from an anonymous donor. In turn, one-parent lesbian families would have to be compared with two-parent lesbian families. (Some of these criteria were met by the Californian sperm bank study.)[18] As proper comparisons have to filter out any stresses that might affect the outcomes, mothers must be economically secure, with full social support, no disruptions and their child[ren] reared from birth by lone- mothers or couples who do not separate and have no conflict.

In reality, all other things are rarely equal or controllable. However, samples should have controls or be matched, insofar as this is possible, for factors which may have an independent effect on outcomes – such as parental age, education, and income. However, family structures will themselves differ in the risks and opportunities they extend to growing children. The degree to which children are going to be exposed to, or affected by, different variables may be the result of family circumstances, or virtually inseparable from this. Since two women, or two men, cannot produce a child together, the 'step-parent' effect is bound to be prevalent in lesbian parenting, insofar as the mother has relationships with women unrelated to the child(ren). Should the child(ren) be conceived within a marriage or other heterosexual relationship, there are the unavoidable effects of divorce or separation, where the child(ren) will have spent time with two parents earlier in life. Otherwise, and unavoidably, the parent is going to be a single parent, with all that this involves.

Communities for children?

Considering that there is no research directly available on 'gay' adoption, this can only be illuminated obliquely. It is likely that some lesbian adoptions are hidden in the samples of single person adoptions. Even then, it is usually difficult to access the relative success of single person and couple adoptions, due to the way in which carers are hand-picked and matched to particular children. In turn, carers may have continuing support services in the management of the increasingly difficult children with special needs who now enter adoption. There may be advantages to placement with a single woman for particular children. However, even if there were isolated cases where it was shown that a child benefited from a placement with, for example, older lesbians, that does not create a principle for public policy. For severely sexually or physically abused children it would provide for a more or less guaranteed absence of a male presence in the home, with which the child may not be able to cope. Some 'attachment disordered' children who develop patterns of 'divide and rule' to survive in their original families or in care may undermine their adoptive parents' relationships as much as their own placement by manipulating one parent against the other.[19]

On the whole, married couples, families with prior adoptive experience, and couples where both spouses are equally committed, have fewer placement breakdowns.[20] Having a natural child close in years, and thus in needs, to the adopted child increases the risk of breakdown, making childless couples better with sibling groups and so forth. Placement with a single woman may be especially difficult with boys, who tend to have more adjustment problems. A study of the adoptions of 73 older, disturbed children, found that of the six boys placed with single women, five of these placements disrupted.[21]

Adopted children are often 'harder to rear' when compared to non-adopted children, due to genetic vulnerabilities and adverse early environments, but adoptive parents tend to be more resourceful than others. They are well prepared for parenthood and have greater personal and social resources – having to prove their ability as parents before undertaking the task. Adopting couples are more likely to have better familial and marital functioning, to be more adaptable and cohesive compared to other two-parent families, and to be more integrated with their families of origin and their in-laws and more likely to have shared friends.[22] Married couples who adopt are less likely to divorce than the general population of married couples.[23] Not least, adopted children do so much better than their comparable peers in institutions, foster homes and those left with their original parents, because adopters are keen to rear a child.[24] Success with late and special needs adoptions lies in the satisfaction parents get from their relationship with the child, their mutual identification and the occupation of parenthood itself as a lifelong interest and vocation. This gives satisfaction in helping a child to develop, through the successful navigation of the problems of child rearing and the appreciation of the simple pleasures of life.[25]

The success of adoption, like that of parenting generally, is related to support from the wider family and friends. Marriage creates affiliate and integrative patterns, and a personal social security system, or network of obligated kin, which is multigenerational. Parents who experience marital breakdown are less likely to feel supported by relatives compared with intact families, and their own obligations to in-laws are substantially weakened after divorce.[26] Children of divorced families report weaker relationships with both parents in adulthood; are less likely to perceive parents as sources of emergency assistance, and report receiving less help.[27]

Children with a lone-parent may not only lack the opportunity to live with another reliable adult of the opposite sex over a long period of time, but may generally have less and weaker links with kin and family friends. Much is made, in lone- and lesbian-parenting manuals, of recruiting or cultivating an 'extended' family made up of friends and acquaintances or past partners. However, as found in longitudinal studies of adoption, few lone women make permanent partnerships, and friends of singles are not always inclined to be as positive about adoption as those of couples, male friends tend to 'disappear' and male relatives die off.[28]

Paedophobia

There is a frequent complaint to the effect that: "The lesbian and gay club scene does not cater to the needs of lesbian or gay parents and rarely, if ever, acknowledges their existence, and some are still shocked to discover that lesbians and gay men do have children."[29] It must be borne in mind that, whatever the interests, inclinations and attributes of particular individuals, "...most homosexuals do not have and do not want children[and] the homosexual associates of homosexual parents would appear to provide less social support to the children of homosexuals than would be provided by the associates of heterosexual parents who usually want and have children."[30] Most male homosexuals have little interest in children. The attention and resources these demand are at odds with a narcissistic existence dedicated to pleasure, sex and style. Jake Arnott, homosexual writer, speaks for many when he says how "...he fits in well with his four siblings and their families, without wanting that life for himself. 'Sure, some gay men want to be fathers but actually a lot of them don't'."[31] This is underlined by the US city sample of the extent of gay parenting, where 70 per cent of homosexual men said that they did not want to have children, compared to 24 per cent of heterosexuals and nearly 50 per cent of bisexuals (the figures for women are similar).[32] Two researchers and 'gay fathers' admit that "...gay culture is singles oriented with individuals often having few long-term commitments, few if any financial responsibilities for others, and heavy emphasis on personal freedom and autonomy". They also describe how common it is for gay fathers to experience

"...discrimination and rejection from other gays who are not fathers because of these restrictions to freedom and the lack of understanding if not devaluation of the place of children in one's life...liaisons present unusual strains due to feelings of jealousy toward the children often experienced by their male partner, and the knowledge that the gay father typically will maintain strong if not preferential ties and loyalties to his children."[33]

Others complain that the lesbian community is not supportive of mothers and how sons "are often treated as second class people".[34] Laura Lott-Whitehead and Carol T. Tully, remark that: "the most surprising finding of the[ir] study" was the way in which women "did admit to curtailing lesbian activity because of parenting" given an "anti-family, anti-children slant...within the very communities they had counted on for emotional, social and political alliance." Significantly:

"Although the community seemed to think it was cool to adopt, I received very little concrete support and most groups preferred not to have a little kid hanging around. Most lesbians were very unfamiliar with normal childhood behaviour."[35]

It is also reported in Lott-Whitehead and Tully's study of lesbian families how, despite the respondents being "...well educated white women with high incomes", most had moderately to very high stress scores. It is smartly concluded that the "...most obvious hypothesis is that those high levels are due to societal prejudice/homophobia." [36] But most of the families were lone-parented, and in other research, lone-motherhood and psychological stress are closely correlated. Even in a study of financially secure single heterosexual mothers who had raised their children since birth without a male partner, the more negative outcomes for the children were associated with the low levels of social support and high level of stress experienced by the mothers. [37] In Lott-Whitehead and Tully's study, the lesbian mothers with lower stress levels had good grandparent and other relative support, underlining how stress is buffeted by supportive networks. In contrast, lesbian circles were explicitly unsupportive of motherhood.[38] The problem is obviously more the paedophobia of gay and lesbian communities than the homophobia of the wider society. In the UK a 'gay' foster carer reports how:

> "I think fostering has prevented me having relationships in the past. One time I was seeing someone and one lad I was looking after got hold of this man's phone number and made a sexually abusive phone call to him. It was awful and had to be looked into and the lad was moved... Some gay men run a mile when they hear that you are a foster carer. I usually tell people I meet, in the pub or whatever, but gay men are just not used to having kids around. Some are very self-orientated, just wanting to be out on the scene and in the clubs, and they're just not used to having to put the needs of two little people first. Also, I don't get to go out as much and it's hard to make plans very far in advance. If I do meet someone, I've got to go through all that stuff about explaining why the children are so demanding and why their behaviour can be so difficult sometimes, and that's a lot to expect a partner to take on board."[39]

Instability

We need to consider not only the lack of extended family and community support for lesbian and homosexual parenting, but the impact of relationship transitions and step-parenthood. These have a particular relevance to homosexual parenting, given that a child is invariably going to be unrelated to one partner, and given the high rates of partnership turnover among homosexuals. Homosexual relations – certainly in the case of men – are often transient, and marked by a very high degree of promiscuity. The most 'stable' of 'gay partnerships' are ones where there is an arrangement between the two to have sex with third parties on the side, while maintaining a permanent living arrangement, so that the "...socio-sexual organisation of gay men...suggest a structure predominantly comprised of regular couples who are also having casual sexual partners".[40] Sexual inclusivity is intrinsic to gay culture and identity, where "...non-exclusive relationships are, for many men, simply more fulfilling than monogamous ones...".[41] Other work shows that nearly a quarter of male homosexuals had between 10 and 100 partners over five years, compared to just over five per cent of heterosexuals (who were sexually active).[42] The same study showed that women in general have fewer sexual partners than men, but revealed that of those who were sexually active, 38 per cent of lesbians and 26 per cent of heterosexual women had more than one partner in the past five years.[43] Project SIGMA, the largest UK study into the sexual behaviour of homosexual and bisexual men, operating from a 'pro-gay' standpoint, found that the median length of a regular relationship was 21 months (although this did not mean that it was sexually monogamous). The majority had casual partners, the median number being seven a year, but men using 'cottages' [public lavatories] averaged 30. Over a quarter of the sample – in each case – met casual partners through cruising or cottaging and a half – in each case – in pubs or clubs.[44] Another study carried out by homosexual researchers, found that only seven out of 156 men maintained monogamy, and none out of the 95 who had been together for more than five years.[45]

This all suggests that children living with homosexuals – particularly male homosexuals – are more likely to face high prospects of repeated family disruption, or multiple family transitions and exposure to high stranger levels in the home, compared to those living with heterosexuals. The research has long indicated an "...absence of a remarriage benefit...[for] children in stepfamily households"[46] and the situation is unlikely to be different for pairings among homosexuals. Many studies show as high or higher problem rates and adverse outcomes for children in step-father families as for those of lone-parents. Overall the general well being of step-children tends to be closer to children of lone-parents than to those with two original parents. In one prominent US three-wave study,[47] adolescent children in divorced lone-mother families and step-families formed through remarriage consistently scored less well for behaviour, competence and education than comparable children whose parents were in stable marriages. Over a two-year study period there was a decline in positive relationships between adolescents and step-fathers, and increases in withdrawal and antisocial behaviour towards mothers. Data from the 1987-88 National Survey of Families[48] shows how children who live in step-father households are twice as likely to have behaviour problems at school as children who live with biological mothers and fathers (26 per cent vs. 11 per cent). The Western Australian Child Health Survey, involving 2,737 children aged between four and 16, focused on three primary spheres of influence on children's development: family, school, and community. Three risk factors – relating to discipline style, family type, and the level of discord in the household – were able to predict more than 80 per cent of children with mental health problems. A child in a step-family was 2.4 times more likely and a child with one parent 2.5 times more likely to have problems than a child with an intact, original family. High discord made it 1.7 times more likely. If a child is exposed to more than one of these risk factors, the likelihood of them having problems multiplies accordingly.[49]

Major longitudinal studies in the UK and US suggest that boys with step-parents are as or more likely to be involved with crime than boys of lone-mothers.[50] For example: the US National Longitudinal Survey of Youth shows how boys raised outside of an intact marriage are, on average, more than twice as likely as other boys to go to jail. The rate rises three-fold for boys with step-parents, to the same level as that for boys without parents at all, although the latter tend to come from far more difficult circumstances.[51] Also girls from step-families were more likely to drop out of school, to leave home early and become teen-parents than those with lone-mothers.[52]

Homelessness

Family structure affects the make-up of the homeless population, predominantly through the 'step-parent effect'. According to the National Child Development Study, the odds are that a young man from a step-family or with a lone-father will leave home for negative reasons at a rate three to six times higher than if he had an intact family.[53] Most leave their parental home because of conflict and only a small minority of young people choose to leave.[54] Joan Smith and her colleagues' in-depth study of homeless people aged 16 to 25 in 1998,[55] found that two-thirds had experienced family breakdown, often combined with the arrival of a step-parent or mother's boyfriend(s) and periods in care (nearly a quarter had spent time in care). Young people reported violence and sexual abuse, as well as abandonment or physical abuse from a birth parent in reconstituted households, or neglect from lone-mothers with a series of boyfriends.[56] In such households: "the obligation to support may simply not be there, whatever the combined earnings of the couple... One of the major causes of youth homelessness is [now] the...re-marriage or re-partnering of their own parents."[57] This is further underlined by a recent Children's Society report on runaways from home and care. Under 16s were three times more likely to run away from step-families, and twice as likely to run away from a lone-parent, than were children living with both birth parents.[58] It is obviously wrong "to assume that reconstituted households continue to have the same commitment to long-term support of young people" as those with the original parents together.[59] At the very least, "the family script alters and young people feel excluded", with obligations in reconstituted households downgraded.[60] Effects of 're-partnering' persist well into adulthood, since young adult offspring receive less assistance from step-families than from continuously intact families.[61] Not least, going back to the parent's home is not an option for those who find themselves with housing problems.[62]

The formation of a step-family is associated with greater stress in nearly all family subsystems, whether between parent and step-parent, step-parent and step-child, or between step-siblings.[63] Accounts abound of relatively loveless, unsatisfying and ambivalent step-relationships; lacking in warmth and support compared to biological relationships[64] and becoming more, not less, negative over time. Step-families tend to be less cohesive than intact families, parental investment is more likely to be withheld, and those involved see their relationships as less dependable in terms of material and emotional support than genetic parent/child relationships.[65] As underlined by White's study of the long-term effects on family solidarity in lone-parent and step-parent families, even more "...pervasive than reports of conflict...are reports of disengagement. Nearly every observer describes step-parents' [typical] parenting style as disengaged." In turn "...perhaps one-fourth to one-third of adolescent step-children disengage themselves emotionally and physically from their step-family".[66]

It is unlikely that homosexual 'co-parents' are going to cope any better with the difficulties or drawbacks of step-parenting, although such arrangements are inherently more likely for children with homosexuals compared to heterosexuals. All societies are pessimistic about childrearing by non-relatives. Parental love is an onerous commitment and it cannot be fully engaged just by pairing up with someone who already has dependent children. The problem is that "the 'ambiguity' of the step-parent's situation does not reside in society's failure to define his role, but in genuine conflicts of interest within the step-family."[67]

Family process not family structure?

Studies of homosexual parenting, in supposedly showing how fine the children turn out, are also held to demonstrate how: "children's well being is more a functioning of parenting and relationship processes within the family (i.e. family interactions and processes) than it is a function of household composition or demographic factors".[68] This move is typically used to deny the evidence now available that the married, two-parent family provides the most successful child rearing environment, and therefore, that lone-parenting, unwed motherhood, step-parenting, divorce and casual, revolving associations have little or no disadvantages for children. With sexual orientation now added to the list, so it

"…might be argued that certain kinds of family interactions, processes, and relationships are beneficial for children's development, but that parents need not be heterosexual to provide them. In other words, variables related to family processes (e.g., qualities of relationships) may be more important predictors of child adjustment than are variables related to family structure (e.g., sexual orientation, number of parents in the home)."[69]

Thus while the significance "of sensitive parenting in creating secure relationships" was noted by one study, it then claimed that this "does not stipulate the necessity of any particular family constellation or structure."[70]

However, while family structure on its own is not a predictor of child development, it is often a proxy for those factors that directly affect children's well-being. Process and structure are two closely interrelated aspects of family life, and family structure influences child development through its impact on family processes. These might be the characteristics of the relations that accompany marital dissolution or intermittent cohabitation (for example, decreased attention, affection and communication), as well as the 'task overload' of lone-parents. Those who speak of 'processes' almost suggest that the making and breaking of significant relationships are irrelevant, as long as someone is making up any shortfall in some requisite input. As seen above, differences in family processes associated with parental separation and step-parenting are critical for the child's social and emotional development. To take one example it is easy to claim that once the quality of relationships with parents and their willingness to supervise their children are taken into account, the influence of family structure on delinquency disappears. However, two concerned adults are, on average, more likely to provide adequate supervision than one. A lone-parent may be less capable of providing supervision, and *if* poor supervision is linked to delinquency, there is an unavoidable link between disrupted families and criminality.[71] The continuance, let alone quality, of a child's relationship with a natural parent is affected by whether they are divorced or if the child ever knew one parent from the beginning. An intact marriage therefore strongly affects the probability that a child will have a good relationship with a father. Fathers who live in separate households often have a low level of involvement with their children, become less altruistic towards, or less closely identified with them over time, less aware of their needs, and less willing to share their income with them.

Much available research on the links between family structure, process and child outcomes has a bearing on lesbian and 'gay' parenting – as already seen in relation to some of the available research relating to step-parenting and intergenerational family patterns. The 1,400 older boys and young men in the Tomorrow's Men project give us some idea of the particular relevance of fathers.[72] A Can-do attitude amongst boys – involving a positive attitude to life, combining confidence, optimism and self-motivation – is linked to school ethos, as well as with a positive parenting style (which is empathic and emotionally supportive), high family togetherness and highly involved fathering. While Low Can-do girls are significantly less able to turn to their mothers as confidantes and supporters, boys who are not doing so well tend to receive low level fathering. Significant associations exist between the degree to which a boy has an involved father (in the sense of spending time with a son, talking about worries and showing interest in schoolwork) and positive behaviour and personal outcomes. Can-do boys commonly report Highly Involved Men (HIM) in their lives, so that 91 per cent with HIM are Can-do boys. But 72 per cent of those with Dad Deficit (DD) are Low Can-do boys. Compared with boys with DD, those with high level fathering are more likely to care about social and community issues, to have strong ideas of right and wrong, and to consider or imagine themselves as a father one day. Young men with HIM are also more optimistic than boys with DD about their own life opportunities and the prospects of achieving their goals. Only a quarter of those boys with Highly Involved Men in their lives have one or more problems (of depression, being in trouble with the police and being anti-school), compared with two thirds of those with a Dad Deficit where more than one in 10 have all three.

Similar associations between positive paternal engagement and outcomes in children aged five to 18 in two-parent families, emerged from the US National Survey of Families and Households.[73] For both boys and girls, high positive paternal engagement is highly associated with lower levels of behaviour and psychiatric troubles, and better sociability. In boys, it also predicted fewer school behaviour problems. (These results took account of positive maternal engagement, race and socio-economic variables, like parental income, status and education).

The Katz study showed that among boys who say that they have a bad relationship with their fathers, those admitting to having offended are double those of young people who claimed to have had a good relationship. To be sure, for that minority who have experienced parental separation "communication and contact, reassurance and stability will have an influence in limiting the likelihood of long term difficulties." However, much "communication and contact, reassurance and stability" stems from having an intact family in the first place.[74]

Endnotes:

[1]   Flaks D K, Ficher I, Masterpasqua, F and Joseph, G, *Op cit*, pages 105-114

[2]   Stacey, J and Biblarz, T J, *Op cit*, page 175

[3]   Sarantakos, S, *Op cit*, pages 23-31

[4]   *Ibid*, page 29

[5]   Golombok S, Spencer, A and Rutter, M, *Op cit*, page 560

[6]   In the National Child Development Study step-fathers were considerably less interested in children's school progress than were fathers in unbroken families. Almost twice as many (33 per cent to 18 per cent) were rated as showing little or no interest and only 24 per cent, compared to 45 per cent of natural fathers, were very interested, whatever their social class. Moreover, if single or divorced mothers were comparatively uninterested in their children, the same went for remarried mothers, especially when they had sons. (Only 24 per cent were very interested, compared to 43 per cent of mothers in unbroken families.) Step-father families also contained the highest proportion who wanted their children to leave school at the earliest possible opportunity, and had the lowest aspirations when it came to jobs. Social class made no difference in the case of boys.
Ferri, E, *Step Children, A National Study, A Report from the National Child Development Study*, Windsor NFER-Nelson, 1984, pages 58-62

[7]   This difference in investment probably explains the way in which offspring of mothers who remarried had lower educational achievement (by nearly one year) than did those whose mothers did not remarry in the Study of Marital Instability Over the Life Course. Amato, P R and Booth, A, 'Consequences of Parental Divorce and Marital Unhappiness for Adult Well-Being', *Social Forces*, 69(3), 1991, pages 895-914

[8]   Amato, P, *Children in Australian Families: The Growth of Competence*, Prentice Hall, New York, 1987, page 115, 243-244

[9]   Chan R W, Raboy, B and Patterson, C J, *Op cit*, pages 443-457

[10] *Ibid*, page 450, Table 3. Lesbian mothers' ratings of their own children's social competence, internalised problems, and total behaviour problems were slightly better than the heterosexual mothers' rating of their own children. The reverse applied to externalising behaviour problems. For all four comparisons, the heterosexual lovers' ratings of the child were slightly better than the ratings of the child by the lesbian lovers, particularly where total behaviour problems were concerned. Teachers rated the lesbians' children slightly better on internalised problems, but worse for externalised

behaviour problems, total behaviour problems and adaptation.

11 *Ibid*, page 455

12 Golombok S, Tasker, F and Murray, C, 'Children Raised in Fatherless Families from Infancy: Family Relationships and the Socioemotional Development of Children of Lesbian and Single Heterosexual Mothers', *Journal of Child Psychology and Psychiatry* 38(7), 1997, pages 783-791

13 *Ibid*, page 785

14 Biller, H B and Kimpton, J L, 'The Father and School-Aged Child' in Lamb, M E (Ed.) *The Role of the Father in Child Development,* John Wiley & Sons, New York, 1997, pages 143-161

15 Golombok S, Tasker, F and Murray, C, *Op cit*, page 788

16 *Loc cit*

17 *Ibid*, page 789

18 See above: Chan R W, Raboy, B and Patterson, C J, *Op cit*, pages 443-457

19 Triseliotis J, Shireman, J and Hundleby, M, *Op cit*, pages 217, 232

20 Hornby, H C, 'Why Adoptions Disrupt...and What Agencies can do to Prevent it', *Children Today,* 1996, New York, pages 7-11

21 Kagan, R M and Reid, W J, 'Critical Factors in the Adoption of Emotionally Disturbed Youths', *Child Welfare*, 65(1), 1986, pages 63-73

22 Benson P L, Sharma, A R and Roehlkepartain, E C, *Growing Up Adopted,* Search Institute, Minneapolis, 1994, page 43;
Cohen N J, Coyne, J and Duvall, J, 'Adopted and Biological Children in the Clinic: Family, Parental and Child Characteristics', *Journal of Child Psychology and Psychiatry*, 34(4), 1993 pages 545-62; and
Groze, V, *Successful Adoptive Families; A Longitudinal Study of Special Needs Adoption*, Praeger, Connecticut, 1996, pages 37, 113

23 Benson P L, Sharma, A R and Roehlkepartain, E C, *Op cit*, pages 44-45

24 On the success of adopted children see for example: Morgan, P, 'Adoption and the Care of Children' and Whitfield, R, 'Secure Tender Loving Care As Soon As Possible, Please' in Morgan P (Ed.) *Adoption: The Continuing Debate*, The IEA Health and Welfare Unit, 1999, pages 12-15 and 106-107

25 Kadushin, A, *Adopting Older Children*, Columbia University Press, 1970, page 210

26 Coleman M, Ganong, L and Cable, S M, 'Beliefs about Women's Intergenerational Family Obligations to Provide Support Before and After Divorce and Remarriage', *Journal of Marriage and the Family*, 59, 1997, pages 165-176

27 White, L, 'Growing Up with Single Parents and Stepparents: Long Term

Effects on Family Solidarity', *Journal of Marriage and the Family,* 56, 1994, pages 935-948

28 Feigelman, W and Silverman, A, *Chosen Children: New Patterns of Adoptive Relationships,* Praeger, New York, 1983, pages 187-188; and Shireman, J F and Johnson, P R, 'Single-Parent Adoptions: a Longitudinal Study', *Children and Youth Services Review* 7, 1985, pages 321-334

29 Editorial Essay in *Lesbian and Gay Fostering and Adoption – Extraordinary Yet Ordinary,* Hicks, S and McDermott, J (Eds.), *Op cit,* page 156

30 Cameron, P and Cameron, K, 'Homosexual Parents', *Op cit,* page 768

31 Crampton, R, 'Jake's Progress', *Times Review,* 5 February 2000

32 Cameron, P and Cameron, K, 'Homosexual Parents', *Op cit,* page 762

33 Bigner, J J and Bozett, F W, 'Parenting by Gay Fathers' in Bozett, F W and Sussman, M B (Eds.), *Op cit,* page 159

34 Lott-Whitehead L and Tully, C T, 'The Family Lives of Lesbian Mothers', *Smith College Studies in Social Work* 63, 1993, page 273

35 Lott-Whitehead, L and Tully, C T, 'The Family Lives of Lesbian Mothers', in Laird J (Ed.), *Op cit,* pages 255 and 251

36 *Ibid,* page 256

37 Weinraub, M and Gringlas, M B, 'Single Parenthood', in Bornstein, M H (Ed.) *Handbook of Parenting: Vol.3, Status and Social Conditions of Parenting,* Laurence Erlbaum Associates, Mahwah, New Jersey, 1995, pages 78-81

38 Lott-Whitehead, L and Tully, C T, 'The Family Lives of Lesbian Mothers', in Laird, J (Ed.), *Op cit,* pages 254-256

39 Hicks, S and McDermott, J, *Op cit,* page 35

40 Hickson, F C I et al, 'Maintenance of Open Gay Relationships: Some Strategies for Protection against HIV', *AIDS CARE,* 4(4), 1992, page 417

41 *Ibid,* page 410

42 Johnson, A M et al, *Op cit,* pages 212-214. Calculations based on eliminating those who have had no partners in the last five years. The new National Survey of Sexual Attitudes and Lifestyles was published at the time of going to press. See footnote 64 of chapter 3. Johnson, A M et al, 'Sexual Behaviour in Britain: Partnerships, Practices and HIV Risk Behaviours', *The Lancet,* 358, December 2001, pages 1835-1841.

43 *Ibid,* page 213. Calculations based on eliminating those who have had no partners in the last five years.

44 Weatherburn, P et al, *Op cit,* pages 11, 19, 20. (Cruising means picking up casual partners in public places.)

45   McWhirter, D and Mattison, A, *The Male Couple: How Relationships Develop*, Prentice-Hall, 1984, pages 252, 207

46   Hanson T L, McLanahan, S S and Thomson, E, 'Double Jeopardy: Parental Conflict and Stepfamily Outcomes for Children', *Journal of Marriage and the Family*, 58, 1996, page 141

47   Hetherington, M E and Clingempeel, W G, 'Coping With Marital Transitions', *Monographs of the Society for Research in Child Development*, Series 227, 57(2-3), 1992, pages 58-72

48   Hanson T L, McLanahan, S S and Thomson, E, *Op cit*, pages 141-154

49   Silburn S R, Zubrick, S R et al, *Western Australian Child Health Survey: Family and Community Health,* Australian Bureau of Statistics, Perth, Australia, 1996 pages 2, 55, 56;
     Spruijt, E and De Goede, M, *Op cit*, pages 1-16.
     In this major Dutch study of the life-course of 2,500 youngsters aged 15 to 24, those from stable two-parent families had the best results for physical and psychological health, relationships with others and employment, and those with one-parent the worst. The children in step-families fell between, being close to the one-parent children for psychological problems, and closer to the two-parent children in physical, relational and employment matters.

50   Ferri, E, *Op cit*, page 79.
     In the longitudinal Oregon Youth Study, the chances that boys who had been through divorce by the age of 10 would be more anti-social was especially marked where they had step-fathers.
     Capaldi, D M and Patterson, G R, 'Relation of Parental Transitions to Boys' Adjustment Problems': I. A Linear Hypothesis, II. Mothers at Risk for Transitions and Unskilled Parenting', *Developmental Psychology*, 27, (3), 1991, pages 489-504.
     Haurin, R J, 'Patterns of Childhood Residence and the Relation to Young Adult Outcomes', *Journal of Marriage and the Family*, 54, 1992, pages 846-860.
     Similarly, in Laurence Steinberg's survey of 865 American adolescents, youngsters in step-families were just as much at risk for involvement in deviant behaviour as those in lone-parent households:
     Steinberg, L, 'Single Parents, Stepparents, and the Susceptibility of Adolescents to Antisocial Peer Pressure', *Child Development*, 58, 1987, pages 269-275

51   McLanahan, S S and Harper C C, 'Father Absence and Youth Incarceration',

Center for Research on Child Wellbeing Working Paper #99-03, 1998, pages 25-26, 40

52 Kiernan, K E, 'The Impact of Family Disruption in Childhood on Transitions Made in Young Adult Life', *Op cit*, page 213

53 *Ibid*, page 227.

A survey of Scottish young people in the mid-1990s found that nearly a half of under-19s with a step-parent had left home, compared to a third of those who had lived with their birth parents.

Jones, G, *Leaving Home*, Open University Press, Buckingham, 1995, page 48

Strathdee, R, *16 & 17, No Way Back, Homeless sixteen & seventeen year olds in the 90s* London: Centrepoint Soho, 1992, page 11.

Submissions to the Australian Burdekin report on homeless youngsters from numerous refuges and counts in different states showed how these came overwhelmingly from step-families or lone-parent households. Burdekin Report: Report of the National Inquiry into Homeless Children, *Our Homeless Children*, AGPS, Canberra, 1989. Discussed in Tapper, A, *The Family in the Welfare State*, Allen & Unwin and the Australian Institute for Public Policy, Perth, 1990, page 202

54 Smith J, Gilford, S and O'Sullivan, A, *The Family Background of Homeless Young People*, Family Policy Studies Centre, 1998, page 10

55 *Ibid*, page 12

56 A half also experienced mental health problems – depression, self-harm and suicide attempts compared with a third of those from non-disrupted households, and the associated factors were much the same as those which had driven them away from home: 'abuse – sexual, physical verbal – or neglect/rejection by the mother or failure by her to protect them from abuse.' *Ibid*, pages 25, 31, 32

57 *Ibid*, pages 49, 32

58 Rees, G and Rutherford, C, *Homerun: Families and Young Runaways*, The Children's Society, Briefing Paper, 2001, page 1

59 Smith J, Gilford, S and O'Sullivan, A, *Op cit*, page 32

60 *Loc cit*

61 White, L, 'The Effect of Parental Divorce and Remarriage on Parental Support for Adult Children', *Journal of Family Issues*, 13(2), 1992, pages 234-250;

White, L, 'Growing Up with Single Parents and Stepparents: Long-Term Effects on Family Solidarity', *Op cit*, pages 935-48;

Amato, P R and Booth, A, *A Generation at Risk*, *Op cit*, pages 178, 181

[62] In the National Child Development Study, young men with step-parents were three times more likely to be homeless between 23 and 33 years old and having to 'move out of a place... having nowhere permanent to live. Hobcraft, J, *Intergenerational and Life-Course Transmission of Social Exclusion: Influences of Childhood Poverty, Family Disruption, and Contact with the Police*, CASE paper 15, Centre for Analysis of Social Exclusion, London School of Economics, 1998, pages v, 5

[63] White, L K and Booth, A, 'The Quality and Stability of Remarriages: the Role of Stepchildren', *American Sociological Review*, 50, 1985, pages 689-698

[64] Thomson E, McLanahan, S S and Curtin, R B, 'Family Structure, Gender and Parental Socialisation', *Journal of Marriage and the Family,* 54, 1992, pages 368-378

[65] Amato, P, *Children in Australian Families: The Growth of Competence, Op cit*, page 115; Santrock J W, Sitterle, K A and Warshak, R A, 'Parent-Child Relationships in Stepfather Families', in Bronstein, P and Pape Cowan, C (Eds.), *Fatherhood Today: Men's Changing Role in the Family*, John Wiley & Sons, New York, 1988, page 160; Hetherington E M, Stanley-Hagan, M and Anderson, E R, 'Marital Transitions: a Child's Perspective', *American Psychologist* , 44(2), 1989, page 308;
Attempting to explain why children in step-father families did worse than children with their original two parents, and no better than children in lone-mother households, Thomas Hanson, Sara McLanahan, Elizabeth Thomson could not account for the difference in terms of exposure to family conflict, regardless of which measure of child well-being was used. Even when children in the least conflicted step-father households (about 25 per cent of all children in this type of household) were compared with children in their original two-parent households or with lone-mothers with average levels of conflict, the former still did worse on many of the important indicators of well-being. Hanson T L, McLanahan, S S and Thomson, E, *Op cit*, pages 151-154

[66] White, L, 'Growing Up with Single Parents and Stepparents: Long-Term Effects on Family Solidarity', *Op cit*, page 937

[67] Daly, M and Wilson, M, *Homicide,* A De Gruyter, New York, 1988, page 93

[68] Chan R W, Raboy, B and Patterson, C J, *Op cit*, page 454

[69] Patterson, C J, 'Children of Lesbian and Gay Parents', *Op cit*, page 1036

[70] *Ibid*, page 1037

[71] Dornbusch, S M et al, 'Single Parents, Extended Households, and the Control of Adolescents', *Child Development*, 56, 1985, pages 327-341

72 Katz, A, *Leading Lads*, University of Oxford, Department of Applied Social Studies and Research in association with Topman, Young Voice (publisher), undated, chapter 4

73 Mosley, J and Thomson, E, 'Fathering Behavior and Child Outcomes: the Role of Race and Poverty', in Marsiglio, W (Ed.), *Fatherhood: Contemporary Theory, Research, and Social Policy*, Sage Publications, 1995, pages 148-165; see also discussion in Pleck, J H, 'Paternal Involvement: Levels, Sources, and Consequences', in Lamb, M E (Ed.), *Op cit*, page 97

74 Katz, A, *Op cit*, page 9

Chapter 5
Conclusion

Strident claims are now heard that there "are no data to suggest that children who have gay or lesbian parents are different in any aspects of psychological, social, and sexual development from children in heterosexual families"[1], and that:

> "Not a single study has found children of gay or lesbian parents to be disadvantaged in any important way relative to children of heterosexual parents... [T]he evidence to date suggests that home environments provided by gay and lesbian parents are as likely as those provided by heterosexual parents to support and to enable children's psychosocial growth."[2]

These claims cannot be substantiated. Not least, it is difficult to see how non-existent work (on 'gay' fathers, for example) can generate data or constitute a 'study'. While the assertion is that "the sexual orientation of parents or prospective parents should be considered irrelevant" for foster care, and adoption [3] – there is not one published comparative study of the effects of homosexual foster care, or adoption to be found. While the volunteers commonly used may be the best adjusted of any group, one has to agree that, in the studies, "a penumbra of an underlying reality is pushing through..." suggesting that the weight of evidence is not always or typically in the direction the gay lobby would want.[4] If evidence is ever recognised as "not always or typically in the direction the gay lobby would want", there is the same tendency to explain it away, and in the same terms that we often see in other areas of developmental investigation: as when results are unflattering to child care, divorce, step-parenting, cohabitation, unwed or teenage motherhood and so on. Problems or unpromising results are laid at the door of stereotyping, or roles being 'incompletely institutionalised' – so that parents do not know what they are supposed to do – or to society not accepting the equal validity of all 'family forms'. If the outcomes look good, that is a triumph for 'gay' parenting. If outcomes look bad, these are society's fault, or the failure is that of the community for not accepting and supporting a mother's lesbianism.

Recent estimates strongly indicate that the numbers of children with psychosocial disorders has grown over the same time as families have increasingly fractured and fragmented.[5] A correlation is not, of course a causal relationship, except that study after study suggests that children who grow up with both original parents are, on the whole, better off than children living with lone or step-parents[6], whether in terms of health, school performance, intellectual development, behavioural and emotional problems, law-breaking, leaving home early, employment, drug-taking, early pregnancy and other measures. The very recent survey into the mental health of children and adolescents in Great Britain, carried out on behalf of the Department of Health, found that whereas 10 per cent of children aged five to 15 years had a mental disorder, the rates were typically running at double the rate (16 per cent compared to eight per cent), among children in lone-parent as compared to two-parent families, and 15 per cent compared to nine per cent respectively for those with and without a step-family.[7] (These results match those from the Western Australian Child Health Survey.)[8] Those living with cohabiting couples were more likely to have a mental health problem, as distinct from those of married couples (or 11.2 to 7.3). Nearly one in five boys of lone-parents had a mental health problem, with most having a conduct disorder. (For girls, it was one in eight, equally distributed between conduct and emotional problems.) Fifty per cent of children with a mental disorder had at one time seen the separation of their parents, compared with 29 per cent of the sample with no disorder, and 37 per cent of those *with* a mental problem compared to 21 per cent of those *without* lived with a lone-parent.[9]

The effect of family fragmentation on future family formation suggests a dynamic that will progressively increase the prevalence of broken families and, in exposing more children to circumstances likely to have other negative consequences for their development, successively undermine the life chances of future generations.

It is now common to hear the (irresponsible) argument that, since more children are seeing, for example, the break up of their parents, or are experiencing other difficulties, tragedies and disappointments, another one will hardly make a difference. Thus a precedent for loss or suffering, is permission to inflict more, or somehow makes it acceptable. This is a variant of the 'new family forms' argument where – since we have had widowhood, now we can have divorce, and if we have unwed motherhood, we can now have lesbian motherhood. A textbook on lesbian parenting explains how to support your child as she grieves not having a father, telling the parent that: "Children who are adopted may grieve the loss of birth parents; children of divorce may have to deal with losing contact with one parent", so there is hardly anything new or special when "...A.I. [artificial insemination] children of lesbian parents may grieve never knowing their biological father."[10]

Because of so many unknowns and the present state of the evidence, we should be circumspect about extending unrestricted parental relationships and rights to homosexual couples – or heterosexual cohabitees, come to that. Parental fidelity to the relationship that generated the child is a powerfully positive influence in the life of the child.

Even if adoption (or surrogacy) rights were explicitly made available only to male homosexuals in stable, exclusive or long term monogamous relationships, or to lone celibates this would, predictably, soon be under attack as 'homophobic' or insensitive to 'gay culture'. We have seen that "...sexual exclusivity amongst gay men is not a norm...". And since such relationships are inherently unstable, any "endorsement of sexual exclusivity..." within these relationships will be condemned as "neither realistic nor necessary", and any call for it seen as "morally guided".[11]

In the interests of adults

Children who become available for adoption are among the most vulnerable of children, often having endured all manner of deprivation, disruptions and disturbances, and often with poor environmental and/or genetic legacies. Children who are raised by a mother and a father are less likely, on the whole, to suffer in these ways. Just as it is more likely that healthy parents will be around as a child grows up compared to those with serious medical conditions, so policies which give preference to married heterosexuals are loading circumstances in favour of the child – even if, in certain cases, an individual will have special skills or circumstances to match the special needs of the child.

If there is any justification for older people, the obese and smokers, being relatively unfavoured as prospective adopters, then it is because they may have shorter life spans, leaving particularly vulnerable children more likely to be orphaned, or orphaned at a younger age. It is interesting that homosexuality is not raised as a similar risk factor, when the lifespan of homosexuals is, on average, so much shorter than that of heterosexuals. One Canadian study found that life expectancy at age 20 years for homosexual and bisexual men is eight to 20 years less than for all men. If the same pattern of mortality were to continue, estimates are that nearly a half of homosexual and bisexual men currently aged 20 years will not reach 65. [12] Their life expectancy is similar to that experienced by all Canadian men in the early 1870s. These statistics only take into account heightened mortality due to HIV/AIDS, where 95 per cent of Canadian cases occur to bisexual and homosexual men. The impact of HIV/AIDS is likely to be underestimated (by 15-20 per cent). Moreover, other causes of mortality may be higher for homosexual and bisexual men. US data shows that homosexual and bisexual men are 3.4 times more likely to die from suicide than the total US male population. [13]

The published interviews with children suggest that it is often more emotionally difficult and demanding to be raised by homosexuals than in other child rearing environments, and this is likely to set children apart, rather than helping them to integrate socially. Set aside, for one moment, whether or not the real problem is the 'homophobic failure of the community to support lesbianism or the gay orientation'. Will it further the child's rehabilitation, or is it in the interests of their welfare, to add worries about their own sexual orientation, the need to manage secrecy, the fear of ostracism, (with the increased risks of rejection by their peers), and the necessity to carry the burden of their parents' sexual choices, let alone exposing them to the partner-changing which is a common feature of 'gay' life? A child adopted along with her brother by a lesbian aunt, recalls how:

> "I was angry that I was not part of a 'normal' family and could not live a 'normal' life with a 'normal' mother. I wondered what I did to deserve this. Why did my biological mother let a lesbian adopt me?... [M]y brother felt a lack of identification with men. He also felt some rejection due to his gender by some 'radical' lesbians. It felt to me like my brother was taken away from me because my mother was gay...[he was eventually adopted by his biological father] I now had to take responsibility for who my mother was. I had to learn to protect her, and myself, from the harsh reality of society's prejudice... I talked with my sister... We also swore we would never be gay...[but one night] my sister confessed to me that she was dating a woman... Then when I was sixteen, I met and fell in love with a woman. I was

really shocked. I didn't understand how this could happen. Up to that point I had dated men – one relationship lasted a year and a half, and several others spanned months at a time... What I began to understand about being gay was that it was a feeling, rather than a choice I was making... I am involved with the Lesbian/Bisexual Alliance."(Female, aged 21)[14]

Moreover, from the perspective of the 'best interests of the child', if homosexual activity – like intravenous drug use – is life shortening, and morbidity attracting, then children should be placed with parents who, at very least, will not steer them towards this. Homosexual parents seem considerably more likely to raise homosexual children. If people are making judgements about where to place children, then is it possible to ignore the differences between ways of life?

It is suggested that, if lesbian and gay parents are not to be oppressed and there is to be "a more genuinely pluralist approach to family diversity" then we should stop comparing different child rearing conditions or family structures in terms of their outcomes for children and just accept that these will be different – but equal.[15] Thus rights for adult homosexuals should not depend upon what happens to children or how they turn out.

"It is neither intellectually honest nor politically wise to base a claim for justice on grounds that may prove falsifiable empirically... [T]he case for granting equal rights to nonheterosexual parents should not require finding their children to be identical to those reared by heterosexuals. Nor should it require finding that such children do not encounter distinctive challenges or risks, especially when these derive from social prejudice."[16]

If children are to be placed for adoption irrespective of the evidence and there is no place for moral judgement or standards for children's custody or upbringing where does this leave us? Following this line of argument to its logical conclusion, there is no reason why children cannot be disposed of, enslaved or sacrificed at parental whim.

Much campaigning for homosexual parental rights involves the use of children by activists to make political statements. Instead, as the Stonewall lecturer asserts at one point, the law "...should facilitate the creation of families which have the optimum prospects of success in promoting the interests of family members, both adults and children."[17]

Endnotes:

[1]   Gold, M A et al, *Op cit*, page 357
[2]   Patterson, C J and Redding, R E, 'Lesbian and Gay Families with Children: Implications of Social Science Research for Policy', *Journal of Social Issues*, 52(3), 1996, page 43
[3]   *Loc cit*
[4]   Cameron, P. 'Homosexual Parents: Testing "Common Sense" – a Literature Review Emphasizing the Golombok and Tasker Longitudinal Study of Lesbians Children', *Op cit*, page 318
[5]   Rutter, M and Smith, D J (Eds.), *Psychosocial Disorders in Young People: Time Trends and Their Causes*, John Wiley & Sons, 1995
       For example, chapter 4 pages 67-103, also chapter 5 pages 104-193
[6]   See for example: Booth, A and Dunn, J, (Eds.) *Stepfamilies: Who Benefits? Who Does Not?*, Lawrence Erlbaum Associates, 1994, chapters 1, 5, 6, 8, 13, 17
[7]   Meltzer, H et al, *Op cit*, pages 26-28
[8]   Silburn S R, Zubrick, S R et al, *Op cit*, page 56
[9]   Meltzer, H et al, *Op cit*, pages 27, 37, 62, 102
[10]   Clunis, D M and Green, G D, *Op cit*, page 55
[11]   Hickson, F C I et al, 'Maintenance of Open Gay Relationships: Some Strategies for Protection against HIV', *Op cit*, page 418
[12]   Hogg R S et al, 'Modelling the Impact of HIV Disease on Mortality in Gay and Bisexual Men', *International Journal of Epidemiology*, 26(3), 1997, pages 657-661
[13]   *Ibid*, page 660 citing Hessol, N A, et al 'Impact of HIV Infection on Mortality and Accuracy of AIDS Reporting on Death Certificates', *American Journal of Public Health*, 82, 1992, pages 561-564
[14]   Rafkin, L, *Op cit*, pages 156-161
[15]   Stacey, J and Biblarz, T J, *Op cit*, page 164
[16]   *Ibid*, page 178
[17]   Bailey-Harris, R, *Op cit*, page 562

Bibliography

This bibliography details the main studies that have been quoted.

Review papers which assess the validity of research papers supporting same-sex parenting

Lerner, R and Nagai, A K, 'No Basis: What the Studies Don't Tell Us About Same-Sex Parenting', *Marriage Law Project*, Washington D C, 2001

Belcastro, P A et al, 'A Review of Data Based Studies Addressing the Affects of Homosexual Parenting on Children's Sexual and Social Functioning', *Journal of Divorce and Remarriage,* 20(1/2), 1993

Stacey, J and Biblarz, T J, '(How) does the Sexual Orientation of Parents Matter?', *American Sociological Review*, 66, 2001

Surveys on children, marriage, the family and sexual behaviour and attitudes

† = specifically covering same-sex parenting

Amato, P R and Booth, A, *A Generation at Risk,* Harvard University Press, 1997

Bebbington, A and Miles, J, 'The Background of Children who enter Local Authority Care', *British Journal of Social Work*, 19, 1989

Bumpass L L, Martin, T C and Sweet, J A, 'The Impact of Family Background and Early Marital Factors on Marital Disruption', *Journal of Family Issues,* 12(1), 1991

Burdekin Report: Report of the National Inquiry into Homeless Children, *Our Homeless Children*, AGPS, Canberra, 1989. Discussed in Tapper, A, *The Family in the Welfare State*, Allen & Unwin and the Australian Institute for Public Policy, Perth, 1990

Dawson, D A, 'Family Structure and Children's Health, United States 1988', *Vital and Health Statistics, Series 10, US Department of Health and Human Services*, 1991

Sex and America's Teenagers, Alan Guttmacher Institute, New York and Washington, 1994

Hanson T L, McLanahan, S S and Thomson, E, 'Double Jeopardy: Parental Conflict and Stepfamily Outcomes for Children', *Journal of Marriage and the Family*, 58, 1996

Hetherington, M E and Clingempeel, W G, 'Coping With Marital Transitions', *Monographs of the Society for Research in Child Development*, Series 227, 57(2-3), 1992

Johnson, A M et al, *Sexual Attitudes and Lifestyles*, Blackwell Scientific Publications, Oxford, 1994

Jones, G, *Leaving Home*, Open University Press, Buckingham, 1995

Katz, A, *Leading Lads*, University of Oxford, Department of Applied Social Studies and Research in association with Topman, Young Voice (publisher), undated

Kiernan, K E, 'The Impact of Family Disruption in Childhood on Transitions Made in Young Adult Life', *Population Studies 46*, 1992

Kiernan, K, *The Legacy of Parental Divorce: Social, economic and demographic experiences in adulthood*, CASE paper 1, Centre for Analysis of Social Exclusion, London School of Economics, 1997

† Kirkpatrick M, Smith, C and Roy, R, 'Lesbian Mothers and their Children: A Comparative Survey', *American Journal of Orthopsychiatry*, 51(3), 1981

Laumann E O, Gagnon J H, Michael, R T and Michaels, S, *The Social Organisation of Sexuality: Sexual Practices in the United States*, The University of Chicago Press, 1994

McLanahan, S, 'Family Structure and Dependency: Early Transitions to Female Household Headship', *Demography*, 25(1), 1988

McLanahan, S and Bumpass, L, "Intergenerational Consequences of Family Disruption", *American Journal of Sociology*, 94(1), 1988

Meltzer, H et al, *The Mental Health of Children and Adolescents in Great Britain*, Office for National Statistics, The Stationery Office, London, 2000

Mosley, J and Thomson, E, 'Fathering Behavior and Child Outcomes: the Role of Race and Poverty', in Marsiglio, W (Ed.), *Fatherhood: Contemporary Theory, Research, and Social Policy*, Sage Publications, 1995

Packman J, Randall, J and Jacques, N, *Who Needs Care? Social-Work decisions about Children,* Basil Blackwell, 1986

Rees, G and Rutherford, C, *Homerun: Families and Young Runaways*, The Children's Society, Briefing Paper, 2001

† Riddle, D I, de Lourdes Arguelles, M, 'Children of Gay Parents: Homophobia's Victims' in Stuart, I R and Abt, L E, (Eds.) *Children of Separation and Divorce*, Van Nostrand Reinhold Company, New York, 1981

Rowe J, Cain H, Hundleby, M and Keane, A, *Long-Term Foster Care*, Batsford Academic and Educational in association with British Agencies for Adoption and Fostering London, 1984

Silburn S R, Zubrick, S R et al, *Western Australian Child Health Survey: Family and Community Health,* Australian Bureau of Statistics, Perth, Australia, 1996

Strathdee, R, *16 & 17, No Way Back, Homeless sixteen & seventeen year olds in the 90s* London: Centrepoint Soho, 1992

Thomson E, McLanahan, S S and Curtin, R B, 'Family Structure, Gender and Parental Socialisation', *Journal of Marriage and the Family,* 54, 1992

Tyas, S L and Pederson, L L, 'Psychosocial Factors Related to Adolescent Smoking: a Critical Review of the Literature', *Tobacco Control,* 7(4), 1998

Weatherburn, P et al, *The Sexual Lifestyles of Gay and Bisexual Men in England and Wales,* HMSO, 1992

Wellings, K, *The National Survey of Sexual Attitudes and Lifestyles: Teenage Pregnancy,* Research results, No. 4, Economic and Social Research Council, June 1997

Wertheimer, A and McRae, S, *Family and Household Change in Britain; A Summary of findings from projects in the ESRC Population and Household Change Programme,* Centre for Family and Household Research Oxford, 1999

White, L, 'The Effect of Parental Divorce and Remarriage on Parental Support for Adult Children', *Journal of Family Issues,* 13(2), 1992

White, L, 'Growing Up with Single Parents and Stepparents: Long Term Effects on Family Solidarity', *Journal of Marriage and the Family,* 56, 1994

Studies/ Review papers

† = specifically covering same-sex parenting

Amato, P, *Children in Australian Families; The Growth of Competence*, Prentice Hall, New York, 1987

Amato, P R and Booth, A, 'Consequences of Parental Divorce and Marital Unhappiness for Adult Well-Being', *Social Forces*, 69(3), 1991

Amato, P R, 'Explaining the Intergenerational Transmission of Divorce', *Journal of Marriage and the Family*, 58, 1996

Axinn, W G and Thornton A, 'The Relationship between Cohabitation and Divorce: Selectivity or Casual Influence?' *Demography* 29(3), 1992

† Bailey J M, Bobrow D, Wolfe, M and Mikach, S, 'Sexual Orientation of Adult Sons of Gay Fathers', *Developmental Psychology*, 31(1), 1995

† Barrett, H and Tasker, F, 'Growing up with a Gay Parent: Views of 101 Gay Fathers on their Sons' and Daughters' Experiences', *Educational and Child Psychology*, 18(1), 2001

Benson P L, Sharma, A R and Roehlkepartain, E C, *Growing Up Adopted*, Search Institute, Minneapolis, 1994

† Bigner, J J and Bozett, F W, 'Parenting by Gay Fathers', *Marriage and Family Review*, 14, 1990

Biller, H B and Kimpton, J L, 'The Father and School-Aged Child' in Lamb, M E (Ed.) *The Role of the Father in Child Development*, John Wiley & Sons, New York, 1997

Booth, A and Dunn, J, (Eds.) *Stepfamilies: Who Benefits? Who Does Not?*, Lawrence Erlbaum Associates, 1994

† Bozett, F W, 'Children of Gay Fathers', in Bozett, F W (Ed.) *Gay and Lesbian Parents*, Praeger, New York, 1987

Buchanan, A and Brinke, J T, *What Happened When They Were Grown Up?*, Joseph Rowntree Foundation, 1997

† Cameron, P and Cameron, K, 'Homosexual Parents', *Adolescence* 31(124), Winter 1996

† Cameron, P, 'Homosexual Parents: Their Children Testify', Unpublished paper, Family Research Institute, 1999

† Cameron, P, 'Homosexual Parents: Testing "Common Sense" – a Literature Review emphasizing the Golombok and Tasker Longitudinal Study of Lesbians' Children', *Psychological Reports* 85, 1999

Campbell, S B, 'Behavior Problems in Preschool Children: A Review of Recent Research', *Journal of Child Psychology and Psychiatry*, 36(1), 1995

Capaldi, D M and Patterson, G R, 'Relation of Parental Transitions to Boys' Adjustment Problems': I. A Linear Hypothesis, II. Mothers at Risk for Transitions and Unskilled Parenting', *Developmental Psychology*, 27, (3), 1991

† Chan R W, Raboy, B and Patterson, C J, 'Psychological Adjustment among Children Conceived via Donor Insemination by Lesbian and Heterosexual Mothers', *Child Development*, 69(2), 1998

Cohen N J, Coyne, J and Duvall, J, 'Adopted and Biological Children in the Clinic: Family, Parental and Child Characteristics', *Journal of Child Psychology and Psychiatry*, 34(4), 1993

Coleman M, Ganong, L and Cable, S M, 'Beliefs about Women's Intergenerational Family Obligations to Provide Support Before and After Divorce and Remarriage', *Journal of Marriage and the Family*, 59, 1997

Coplan, P M et al 'Human Immunodeficiency Virus Infection in Mexico City', *American Journal of Epidemiology*, 144(9), 1996

† Cramer, D, 'Gay Parents and Their Children: A Review of Research and Practical Implications', *Journal of Counseling and Development*, 64, 1986

Daly, M and Wilson, M, *Homicide*, A De Gruyter, New York, 1988

Daly, M, and Wilson, M, *The Truth About Cinderella, A Darwinian view of parental love*, Weidenfeld and Nicolson, London, 1998

Dixon, J K, 'The Commencement of Bisexual Activity in Swinging Married Women Over Age Thirty', *Journal of Sex Research* 20(1), 1984

Dornbusch, S M et al, 'Single Parents, Extended Households, and the Control of Adolescents', *Child Development*, 56, 1985

† Dunne, G, *The Different Dimensions of Gay Fatherhood: Exploding the Myths*, London School of Economics Discussion Paper Series, January 2000

Eckert E D, Bouchard T J, Boulen, J and Heston, L L, 'Homosexuality in Monozygotic Twins Reared Apart', *British Journal of Psychiatry*, 148, 1986

Feigelman, W and Silverman, A, *Chosen Children: New Patterns of Adoptive Relationships*, Praeger, New York, 1983

† Fergusson, D M, 'Family Formation, Dissolution and Reformation', *Proceedings of the SSRFC Symposium: New Zealand Families in the Eighties and Nineties*, Canterbury University, 20, November 1987

Ferri, E, *Step Children, A National Study, A Report from the National Child Development Study*, Windsor NFER-Nelson, 1984

† Flaks D K, Ficher I, Masterpasqua, F and Joseph, G, 'Lesbians Choosing Motherhood: A Comparative Study of Lesbian and Heterosexual Parents and their Children', *Developmental Psychology* 31(1), 1995

Freund K, Heasman G, Racansky, I G and Glancy, G, 'Pedophilia and heterosexuality vs. homosexuality', *Journal of Sex and Marital Therapy*, 10(3), 1984

Frisch, M et al 'Sexually Transmitted Infection as a Cause of Anal Cancer', *New England Journal of Medicine*, 337(19), 1997

Gartner, R, 'Family Structure, Welfare Spending, and Child Homicide in Developed Democracies', *Journal of Marriage and The Family*, 53, 1991

† Gold M A, Perrin E C, Futterman, D and Friedman, S B, 'Children of Gay or Lesbian Parents', *Pediatrics in Review*, 15(9), 1994

† Golombok S, Spencer, A and Rutter, M, 'Children in Lesbian and Single-Parent Households: Psychosexual and Psychiatric appraisal', *Journal of Child Psychology and Psychiatry*, 24(4), 1983

† Golombok, S and Tasker, F 'Children in Lesbian and Gay Families: Theories and Evidence', *Annual Review of Sex Research* 5, 1994

† Golombok, S and Tasker, F, 'Do Parents Influence the Sexual Orientation of Their Children? Findings From a Longitudinal Study of Lesbian Families', *Developmental Psychology*, 32(1), 1996

† Golombok S, Tasker, F and Murray, C, 'Children Raised in Fatherless Families from Infancy: Family Relationships and the Socioemotional Development of Children of Lesbian and Single Heterosexual Mothers', *Journal of Child Psychology and Psychiatry*, 38(7), 1997

Gordon, M, and Creighton, S J, 'Natal and Non-natal Fathers as Sexual Abusers in the United Kingdom: a Comparative Analysis', *Journal of Marriage and the Family*, 50, 1988

† Gottman, J S, 'Children of Gay and Lesbian Parents', in Bozett, F W and Sussman, M B (Eds.) *Homosexuality and Family Relations*, The Haworth Press, New York, 1990

† Green, R, 'Sexual Identity of 37 Children Raised by Homosexual or Transsexual Parents', *American Journal of Psychiatry*, 135(6), 1978

† Green, R et al 'Lesbian Mothers and their Children: A Comparison with Solo Parent Heterosexual Mothers and Their Children', *Archives of Sexual Behaviour*, 15, 1986

Groze, V, *Successful Adoptive Families; A Longitudinal Study of Special Needs Adoption*, Praeger, Connecticut, 1996

Grubin, D, *Sex Offending Against Children: Understanding the Risk*, Home Office, Police Research Series, Paper 99, 1998

Hall, D R, 'Marriage as a Pure Relationship: Exploring the Link Between Premarital Cohabitation and Divorce in Canada', *Journal of Comparative Family Studies*, 27 (1), Spring 1996

† Hartman, A, 'The Long Road to Equality: Lesbians and Social Policy', in Laird J (Ed.) *Lesbians and Lesbian Families*, Columbia University Press, New York, 1999

Haurin, R J, 'Patterns of Childhood Residence and the Relation to Young Adult Outcomes', *Journal of Marriage and the Family*, 54, 1992

† Hays, D and Samuels, A, 'Heterosexual Women's Perceptions of Their Marriages to Bisexual or Homosexual Men' in Bozett F W (Ed.) *Homosexuality and the Family*, The Haworth Press, New York, 1989

Hessol, N A, et al 'Impact of HIV Infection on Mortality and Accuracy of AIDS Reporting on Death Certificates', *American Journal of Public Health*, 82, 1992

Hetherington E M, Stanley-Hagan, M and Anderson, E R, 'Marital Transitions: a Child's Perspective', *American Psychologist*, 44(2), 1989

† Editorial Essay in *Lesbian and Gay Fostering and Adoption-Extraordinary Yet Ordinary*, Hicks, S and McDermott, J (Eds.), Jessica Kingsley Publications, London, 1999

Hickson, F C I et al, 'Maintenance of Open Gay Relationships: Some Strategies for Protection against HIV', *AIDS CARE*, 4(4), 1992

Hickson, F C I et al, 'Gay Men as Victims of Nonconsensual Sex', *Archives of Sexual Behaviour*, 23(3), 1994

Hobcraft, J, *Intergenerational and Life-Course Transmission of Social Exclusion: Influences of Childhood Poverty, Family Disruption, and Contact with the Police*, CASE paper 15, Centre for Analysis of Social Exclusion, London School of Economics, 1998

† Hoeffer, B 'Children's Acquisition of Sex-Role Behavior', *American Journal of Orthopsychiatry*, 51, 1981

Hogg R S et al, 'Modelling the Impact of HIV Disease on Mortality in Gay and Bisexual Men', *International Journal of Epidemiology*, 26(3), 1997

Hornby, H C, 'Why Adoptions Disrupt...and What Agencies can do to Prevent it', *Children Today*, 1996

Hubbard, R and Wald, E, *Exploding the Gene Myth*, Beacon Press, Boston, 1993

† Javaid, G A, 'The Children of Homosexual and Heterosexual Single Mothers', *Child Psychiatry and Human Development*, 23(4), Summer 1993

Johnson, R L and Shrier, D K, 'Sexual Victimisation of Boys: Experience at an Adolescent Medicine Clinic', *Journal of Adolescent Health Care*, 6, 1985

Jones, L, 'Unemployment and Child Abuse', *Families in Society: The Journal of Contemporary Human Services*, 1990

Joshi, H et al, *Children 5-16 Research Briefing No 6*, January 2000, Economic and Social Research Council, University of Hull

Kadushin, A, *Adopting Older Children*, Columbia University Press, 1970

Kagan, R M and Reid, W J, 'Critical Factors in the Adoption of Emotionally Disturbed Youths', *Child Welfare*, 65(1), 1986

† Kirkpatrick, M, 'Clinical Implications of Lesbian Mother Studies', *Journal of Homosexuality*, 14(1-2), 1987

† Koepke, L et al, 'Relationship Quality in a Sample of Lesbian Couples with Children and Child-free Lesbian Couples', *Family Relations*, 41, 1992

Lempers J D, Clark-Lempers, D and Simons, R L, 'Economic

Hardship, Parenting and Distress in Adolescence', *Child Development*, 60, 1989

† Lewis, K G, 'Children of Lesbians: their Point of View', *Social Work*, 25(4), 1980

† Logan, B, 'A submission, with special reference to de facto & same-sex couples, on the Law Commission's "Adoption: options for Reform"', *New Zealand Education Development Foundation*, Preliminary Paper 38, 18 January 2000

† Lott-Whitehead L and Tully, C T, 'The Family Lives of Lesbian Mothers', *Smith College Studies in Social Work 63*, 1993

† Lott-Whitehead, L and Tully, C T, 'The Family Lives of Lesbian Mothers', in Laird J (Ed.) *Lesbians and Lesbian Families*, Columbia University Press, New York, 1999

McLanahan, S S and Harper C C, 'Father Absence and Youth Incarceration', *Center for Research on Child Wellbeing Working Paper #99-03*, 1998

McWhirter, D and Mattison, A, *The Male Couple: How Relationships Develop, Prentice-Hall*, 1984

Margolin, L, 'Child Abuse by Mothers' Boyfriends: Why the Overrepresentation?', *Child Abuse and Neglect*, 16, 1992

† Miller, B, 'Gay Fathers and Their Children', *The Family Coordinator*, 28, 1979

† Miller J A, Jacobsen, R B and Bigner, J J, 'The Child's Home Environment for Lesbian vs. Heterosexual Mothers: A Neglected Area of Research', *Journal of Homosexuality*, 7(1), 1981

† O'Connell, A, 'Voices from the Heart: The Developmental Impact of a Mother's Lesbianism on her Adolescent Children', in Laird J (Ed.) *Lesbians and Lesbian Families*, Columbia University Press, New York, 1999

† Patterson, C J, 'Children of Lesbian and Gay Parents', *Child Development*, 63, 1992

† Patterson, C J and Redding, R E, 'Lesbian and Gay Families with Children: Implications of Social Science Research for Policy', *Journal of Social Issues*, 52(3), 1996

† Pennington, S B, 'Children of Lesbian Mothers', in Bozett, F W (Ed.) *Gay and Lesbian Parents*, Praeger, New York, 1987

Pleck, J H, 'Paternal Involvement: Levels, Sources, and Consequences', in Lamb, M E (Ed.), *The Role of the Father in Child Development*, John Wiley & Sons, New York, 1997

† Rae, G, '"Therapy with a Lesbian Stepfamily with an Electively Mute Child": A Comment', *Journal of Family Psychotherapy*, 6(1), 1995

† Rafkin, L, *Different Mothers: Sons and Daughters of Lesbians Talk about their Lives*, Cleis Press, Pittsburgh, 1990

Remafedi G, Resnick M, Blum, R, and Harris, L, 'Demography of Sexual Orientation in Adolescents', *Pediatrics*, 89(4), 1992

Richman N, Stevenson, J and Graham, P J, *Pre-school to School: a Behavioural Study*, Academic Press, London, 1982

Rutter, M and Smith, D J (Eds.), *Psychosocial Disorders in Young People: Time Trends and Their Causes*, John Wiley & Sons, 1995

† Saffron, L, *What About the Children? Sons and Daughters of Lesbian and Gay Parents talk about their Lives*, Cassell, London, 1996

Santrock J W, Sitterle, K A and Warshak, R A, 'Parent-Child Relationships in Stepfather Families', in Bronstein, P and Pape Cowan, C (Eds.), *Fatherhood Today: Men's Changing Role in the Family*, John Wiley & Sons, New York, 1988

† Sarantakos, S, 'Children in Three Contexts: Family, Education and Social Development', *Children Australia*, 21(3), 1996

Schwarz, M F and Masters, W H, 'The Masters and Johnson Treatment Program for Dissatisfied Homosexual Men', *American Journal of Psychiatry*, 141(2), 1984

Shireman, J F and Johnson, P R, 'Single-Parent Adoptions: a Longitudinal Study', *Children and Youth Services Review 7*, 1985

Skinner, W F, 'The Prevalence and Demographic Predictors of Illicit and Licit Drug Use among Lesbians and Gay Men', *American Journal of Public Health*, 84 (8), 1994

Smith J, Gilford, S and O'Sullivan, A, *The Family Background of Homeless Young People,* Family Policy Studies Centre, 1998

Smith, T W, *Adult Sexual Behaviour in 1989: Number of Partners, Frequency and Risk. GSS Topical report No. 18*, NORC, University of Chicago, 1990

Sohn, N and Robilotti, J G, 'The Gay Bowel Syndrome', *American Journal of Gastroenterology*, 67(5), 1977

Spruijt, E and De Goede, M, 'Changing Family Structures and Adolescent Well-being in the Netherlands', *International Journal of Law, Policy and the Family*, 10, 1996

Steinberg, L, 'Single Parents, Stepparents, and the Susceptibility of Adolescents to Antisocial Peer Pressure', *Child Development*, 58, 1987

Takeuchi D T, Williams, D R and Adair, R K, 'Economic Stress in the Family and Children's Emotional and Behavioural Problems', *Journal of Marriage and the Family*, 53, 1991

† Tasker, F and Golombok, S, 'Adults Raised as Children in Lesbian Families', *American Journal of Orthopsychiatry*, 65(2), 1995

† Tasker, F and Golombok, S, *Growing Up in a Lesbian Family*, The Guilford Press, London, 1997

Thornton, A and Camburn, D, 'The Influence of the Family on Premarital Sexual Attitudes and Behavior', *Demography*, 24(3), 1987

Triseliotis J, Shireman, J and Hundleby, M, *Adoption: Theory, Policy and Practice*, Cassell, London, 1997

Van Wyk, P H and Geist, C S, 'Psychosocial Development of Heterosexual, Bisexual, and Homosexual Behaviour', *Archives of Sexual Behaviour*, 13(6), 1984

† Weeks J, Donovan, C and Heaphy, B, *Families of Choice: The Structure and Meanings of Non Heterosexual Relationships*, Research Results, No 6, Economic and Social Research Council, 1997

Weinraub, M and Gringlas, M B, 'Single Parenthood', in Bornstein, M H (Ed.) *Handbook of Parenting: Vol.3, Status and Social Conditions of Parenting*, Laurence Erlbaum Associates, Mahwah, New Jersey, 1995

White, L K and Booth, A, 'The Quality and Stability of Remarriages: the Role of Stepchildren', *American Sociological Review*, 50, 1985

† Wyers, N L, 'Homosexuality in the Family: Lesbian and Gay Spouses', *Social Work*, 32(2), 1987

Index

C

permanent, 109
're-partnering', 114
same-sex, 24-27, 36, 50, 54, 76, 79-80,
    82, 104, 109, 110-111
Patterson, Charlotte J., 53, 79
Pro-gay research, 47, 51-53, 57-58, 75-77
Promiscuity, 26, 85, 111
Public policy, 28, 42, 47, 53, 57, 61, 107

R

Rafkin, Louise, 74
Rape
    heterosexual, 46
    homosexual, 46, 64
Registered Partnerships, 24-25
Relationships
    adolescent-stepfather, 112
    disrupted family, 35, 104, 117
    egalitarian, 27
    father-son, 81, 117
    family, 50, 104-105
    fluid, 27-29, 42
    formal, 24-26
    'gay', 76, 84-86
    lesbian, 48-49, 53, 76, 84-86, 110
    marital, 25, 27-29, 31-32, 35, 43-44,
        49, 54, 60, 68, 75, 86-89, 100-101,
        106-108, 113, 115-116, 119, 122,
        124, 129-130
    monogamous, 112, 130
    non-exculsive, 111
    parent-child, 42-44, 94, 103-104, 115
    parent-step-parent, 36, 45, 114-115
    pure, 28, 102
    same-sex, 23-32, 36, 76, 84-86, 89,
        111, 130-132
    serial, 28
    step-parent-step-child, 36, 45, 71, 101,
        111-117, 128
Remarriage, see Marriage
Reproduction

artificial insemination, 25, 129
assisted, 23
donor insemination, 23, 31, 36, 104
fertility treatment, 49
methods of procreation, 102
sperm donor, 36
technological developments, 27-28
Research
    assessment scales
        parents', 68, 103
        teachers', 68-69
    defective, 52, 67
    design, 47, 52-53, 67
    epidemiological studies, 68
    faulty assessment, 71
    hypothesis, 50-52, 110
    meta-analysis, 52
    null hypothesis, 51
    population estimates, 56
    population norms, 69, 80, 86
    questionnaires, 35, 68, 79, 104
    reliability, 46, 52, 68
    samples
        controls, 44, 47, 52-59, 67, 76, 88,
            102, 104-106
        matched pairs, 52, 57, 100
        random samples, 35, 56-57, 70
        sample population, 50-51, 54-60,
            67, 69-71, 78, 86-88, 99, 100,
            102-108, 112, 127, 129
        sample size – biased, 57, 71, 105
        sample size – small, 51, 54, 71, 78-
            79
        sampling, 35, 52, 100
        snowballing, 100
    statistical analysis, 51-54, 59, 68-70,
        78-79
    studies
        follow-up, 70-71
        longitudinal, 49, 60, 88, 100, 104,
            109, 113
        observational, 104